Dancing Throughout Mexican History (1325-1910)

Written by:

SANJUANITA MARTÍNEZ-HUNTER

Edited by:

GABRIELA MENDOZA-GARCÍA

ISBN: 0692099662
ISBN-13:9780692099667

DEDICATION

To the two persons I love the most in this world: my mother, Julieta Naranjo Martínez and my husband, Bence Maurice (Reece) Hunter. My lifetime dream became a reality because of your patience, support, encouragement, and love throughout the preparation of this work.

CONTENTS

ACKNOWLEDGMENTS

I would like to express my deepest appreciation to Doctor Aileen Lockhart, for her kind encouragement, invaluable guidance, and whose interest enabled me to continue this work. I am particularly indebted to Doctor Jane Mott, Chairman of the Dance Department and dissertation committee member, for her patience and understanding throughout this work. It has been a great honor to work with both of you ladies.

Grateful acknowledgement is given also to Mrs. Gladys Keeton, Doctor Bert Lyle, and Doctor Rodolfo Rodríguez, for their helpful suggestions and assistance as members of the dissertation committee.

Sincere appreciation is extended to the individuals who made the final manuscript possible. They include Karen Epstein and Cheryl Howry at Papers to Go; Lyndon Henry at Creative Services and the countless friends whose encouragement was invaluable in the completion of this work.

I would like to acknowledge my childhood friend, Mrs. Irma Novoa, for her assistance in all phases of this work. *Mil gracias* Manci!

Finally, a special thank you to my sister, Sara Alicia Mendoza, for her help in reviewing this manuscript,

FOREWORD

My aunt, Sanjuanita Martínez-Hunter (1942-2016), was a vivacious, out-going, and truly unforgettable person. She had a loud, booming voice that towered above the rest in any crowded room. She had so many friends and admirers. Mostly I remember her love of dance. This love of dance ignited a passion for learning. Dance was always a part of her life. As a child she learned Dance from her teachers: Blanche Flores Leyendecker, Elizabeth (Ruby Roy) Galo, Neo Gutiérrez, Eugene Loring, Sevillanito de Triana, Eduardo Cansino Jr., and Frances Gonzalez Scarff. As an adult, she earned her bachelor's, master's, and doctoral degrees in Dance from Texas Women's University. Martínez-Hunter had her own dance studio in Laredo, Texas, started the Monterrey Darlings dance team in Monterrey, Mexico, taught the Lamar Middle School Prancers in Laredo, Texas, and was a Dance faculty at the University of Texas at Austin (UT) where she inspired countless students. She alongside a group of UT students began *El Grupo de Danza y Arte Folklórico de la Universidad de Tejas en Austin* also known as the UT Ballet Folklorico in 1975. Her students Roy Lozano and Michael Carmona were part of the founding members of this group. Roy Lozano would go on to dance with the *Ballet Folklórico de México de Amalia Hernández* and then start his own professional dance company in Austin, Texas called *Roy Lozano's Ballet Folklórico de Tejas*. Michael Carmona would direct the UT Ballet Folklorico for many, many years. Both of her students were my own Dance teachers who were instrumental in my life.

After I finished my own graduate studies, my aunt repeatedly asked me to help her edit and publish her dissertation entitled *The Development of Dance in Mexico 1325-1910*. Unfortunately, I never found the time to help her with this project during her lifetime. Now, after her passing, I have fulfilled her request. This book represents the life's work of Sanjuanita Martínez-Hunter. Throughout the editing process, I have kept the ideas, thoughts and words as written by Martínez-Hunter. I have made a few minor changes to words that are no longer used in the same way in the twenty-first century. I have omitted some paragraphs where new research points her ideas in a different direction. Also, there are two or three ideas that I clarified to make her argument clearer. Besides these changes, the work is entirely hers. All the photographs included in this book are from her personal collection. They document her many contributions to Dance when she was a faculty member at the University of Texas at Austin. This is my way of honoring her.

This book intertwines Mexican history with Dance. In Chapter One entitled "Dance in Pre-Hispanic Mexico: The Aztecs (1325-1519)," Martínez-Hunter narrates the crucial role that Dance played in the lives of the Aztec people. Here, she describes many different types of dances of the Aztecs and how these dances played a role in Aztec social and ceremonial life. In Chapter Two called "Dance in Mexico (1519-1525): The Spanish Influence after the Conquest," Martínez-Hunter details the ways in which the Spanish defeated the Aztecs and how this changed their dances. She writes of the Dance Dramas that arose when the Spanish began to Christianize the Indigenous people. Martínez-Hunter hints at the ways in which these dances retained their Indigenous, ceremonial symbolism while outwardly portraying a Christianizing theme. In Chapter Three entitled, "Dance in Mexico (1525-1810): The Spanish Colonization," her research shows how court dances such as the pavane, sarabande, and the chaconne began in the New World and spread throughout Europe. She also writes of the Indigenous, *mestizo*, Chilean, and African influences on the dances of Mexico. Chapter Four is called, "Dance in Mexico (1810-1910): The Independence of Mexico." Martínez-Hunter writes of the dances during the time of Mexico's Independence from Spain. Here, she notes the African influences on these dances. Martínez-Hunter analyzes the European ballroom dances of this period with their popularity coming from the aristocracy of Mexico. She juxtaposes the European ballroom dances with the dances of the peasant people known as *jarabes* and *sones*. She notes that while the aristocratic ballroom dances were accepted by the elite, many of the *jarabes* were banned throughout Mexico. In so doing, Martínez-Hunter notes that these dances became even more popular as symbols of resistance.

Gabriela Mendoza-Garcia
September 2018

PREFACE

Just below the Rio Grande, the muddy river which marks the southern border of the United States, lies Mexico. Mexico, often described as shaped like a cornucopia, is a country whose colorful history, tradition, and spirit have evolved from ancient Aztec, Mayan, other Indigenous and Spanish cultures.[1] From this rich background and from the influence of some European and African cultures the Mexican dance of today has emerged.

"The oldest and most picturesque cultural aspect of most peoples is its dance. Since remote times, dance has played an essential part in the life of the Mexican people."[2] Mexico possesses an enormously rich dance legacy built upon various ethnic groups: (1) the Pre-Hispanic, (2) the Spanish, (3) the African whose representatives arrived on the southern coastal zones of Mexico during the Spanish colonization, (4) immigrants from European countries which had a direct or indirect influence on the history of Mexico.[3] The dances seen today in Mexico are chiefly from two clearly defined influences: Indigenous and European. These dances reflect the characteristics of

---

[1] Walter Sorell, "Mexico Cornucopia," *Dance Magazine,* August, 1962, p. 48.

[2] Luis Covarrubias, *Regional Dances of Mexico* (México: Fishgrund-Litographia Rekord), p.1.

[3] Electra L. Mompradé and Tonatiúh Gutiérrez, *historia general del arte mexicano: danzas y bailes* populares, trans. Sanjuanita Martínez (México: Editorial Hermes, S. A., 1976), p. 23.

the peoples of Mexico and are colored by the turbulent history of the country.[4]

Dancing has flourished since the days of the Aztec pyramid builders," which occurred between 1325 and 1525.[5] As an integral part of the Pre-Hispanic or Pre-Columbian culture, dance reflected and influenced every aspect of life: political, social, religious, and emotional.[6] Providing historical perspectives and evidence regarding the influence of Pre-Hispanic dance are such sources as the codices, paintings, sculptures, and archeological remains; the original musical instruments still extant from that period, or their reproductions; written descriptions in the chronicles and in writings by those men who took part in the conquest; and the actual Indigenous dances still performed amongst the Indigenous people of modern Mexico. [7]

> ...for the ancient Mexicans there was nothing more vitally important than these motions, these songs, dances....these things assured the regular succession of the seasons, the coming of the rains, the springing of the plants upon which they lived, and the resurrection of the sun...in a perpetual collective effort without which nature itself would be destroyed... the gravest of life's occupations, the most imperative of duties.[8]

[4] Alura Flores Barnes de Angeles, "Mexican Dance," lecture at Mexican Dance Symposium sponsored at the University of Texas at Austin, Texas, March 20, 1979.

[5] Guillermina Dickins, *Dances of Mexico* (Great Britain: Billing and Sons Ltd. Guildford, n.d.), p. 5.

[6] Flores Barnes de Angeles, Mexican Dance Symposium.

[7] Electra L. Mompradé and Tonatiúh Gutiérrez, *historia general del arte mexicano: danzas y bailes* populares, trans. Sanjuanita Martínez (México: Editorial Hermes, S. A., 1976), p. 23.

[8] Jaques Soustelle, *la vida cotidiana de los aztecas,* quoted in *The Ephemeral and the Eternal of Mexican Folk Art,* Vol. II (México: Fondo Editorial de la Plastica Mexicana, 1971), p.392.

The European influence on Mexican dance began at the time of the Spanish Conquest in 1521. The Spanish Conquistadors tried to destroy much of the Indigenous culture of the Aztecs and to replace it with their own culture, customs, and morality.[9] The impact of the conquest and the conversion of the Indigenous people to Christianity led to the development of the dance-dramas whose popular themes included the wars between the Indigenous people and the conquering forces of Cortés and the struggles between good and evil in converting them. Conversion having been achieved, the thematic content became more and more secularized, and other historical events were then reflected in the dance-dramas. Dance-dramas in turn paved the way for masquerade balls, carnival festivals, and farces in burlesque-type theater presentations.

The Spanish Conquest altered dance traditions. From ceremonial dances in which the entire Indigenous community participated, to dances performed by a select few for the purpose of conversion, to the elite courtroom balls of the aristocracy, to the self-expressive dances born in rebellion to oppression, dance eventually ran a full cycle back to folk dance.

In Mexico, each region and each town has invented their own ways of expressing their emotions. Each province has its own special dances, but in many of these can be found the same mixture of cultural ingredients that pervade Mexico's history, folklore, and dance.

[9] Anne Schley Duggan, et. al., *Folk Dances of the United States and Mexico* (New York: A.S. Barnes and Company, 1948), p. 103.

Pictured above are two students of the UT Ballet Folklorico dressed as the *Charro* and the *China Poblana* which is described in Chapter Four. Photo courtesy of the Sanjuanita Martínez-Hunter Collection.

CHAPTER 1: DANCE IN PRE-HISPANIC MEXICO: THE AZTECS (1325-1519)

Prior to the arrival of explorers and settlers from Europe, many different Indigenous tribal groups inhabited the eastern coast of Mexico. While some of these tribes eventually created elaborate cities others lived in a nomadic fashion[1]. The Indigenous tribal group known as the Mexicas, now referred to as the Aztecs, were the last of the groups to develop an expansive society. Before the arrival of the Spaniards in Mexico, the Aztecs, who spoke the Náhuatl language, had developed a powerful empire.[2]

Sources do not agree on where the Aztecs first migrated from. Michael C. Meyer in the book *The Course of Mexican History* places this location in an island off the coast of Nayarit.[3] Alfonso Teja Zabre in *The Guide to the History of Mexico* states that the Aztecs came from Aztatlán or Aztlán, the "land of herons" or the "place where the sun rose."[4] Frederick A. Peterson in *Ancient Mexico* says that the Aztecs may have come from these two places or from one of the following locations: the Lerma River basin, Jalisco, Nayarit, Hidalgo, or Lake

[1]Duggan, p. 100

[2] Victor W. Von Hagen. *The Aztec: Man and Tribe* (New York: New American Library, 1961), pp. 44-47.

[3] Michael C. Meyer and William L. Sherman, *The Course of Mexican History* (New York: Oxford University Press, 1979), p. 5.

[4] Alfonso Teja Zabre, *Guide to the History of Mexico* (Austin: Jenkins Publishing Company, 1969), p. 72.

Pátzcuaro.[5]

Frances Toor in *A Treasury of Mexican Folkways* recounts the legend of how the Aztecs found their homeland. According to tradition, *Huitzilopochtil* (a humming bird wizard),[6] one of the Aztecs' war gods, told the Aztecs to build their city where they sighted a huge eagle clutching a snake in its claws, perched on a *nopal* (cactus), with wings outstretched toward the sunrise. In 1325, after one hundred years of roaming, the Aztecs found the eagle on one of the islands of Lake Texcoco in the Valley of Mexico. They named the site Tenochtitlán, the "place where *nopales* grow."[7] This Aztec capital is now known as Mexico City, named after another war god, *Mexitli*.[8]

A majestic city, Tenochtitlán was graced with aesthetic gardens, palatial houses, and graceful canals. The *Templo Mayor* (Great Temple) dedicated to *Huitzilopochtli* stood in the Zócalo, Mexico City's main plaza. Erected between 1482 and 1485, this temple was connected to schools for priests and warriors, and in these schools music and dance were taught. All aspects of these people's existence, including entertainment and athletics, were interwoven with their religious beliefs. Yet in spite of their disciplined lives, the ruling class of Tenochtitlán lived very comfortably. They wore fine clothes and jewelry handcrafted of gold and precious stones.[9]

Major events in the history of the Aztecs were outlined in Table One. The relationship of these events with the development of dance in Mexico during this period of time is then discussed.

[5] Frederick Peterson, *Ancient Mexico* (New York: G. P. Putnam's Sons, 1961), p. 86.

[6] Victor W. Von Hagen, *The Aztec: Man and Tribe* (New York: New American Library, 1961), p.44.

[7] Frances Toor, *A Treasury of Mexican Folkways* (New York: Crown Publishers, Inc., 1979), p.xxvii.

[8] Nicolas Slonimsky, *Music of Latin America* (New York: Thomas Y. Crowell Company, 1945), p. 214.

[9] Toor, p.xxvii.

Table One
Historical Chronology

1325   The Aztec chief, Tenoch, founded Tenochtitlán, now Mexico City. The Mexica settled and formed the Aztec society.[10]

1376   Prince Acampichtli, ruled the royal city of Tenochtitlán. Although Tenochtitlán was considered a most powerful nation, it was weakened by its dutiful subjection to its national-city, Azcapotzalco.[11]

1396   Huitzilhitl governed Tenochtitlán. The *chinampas* or floating gardens were added to the new agricultural landscape.[12]

1418   Netzahualcóyotl, the young prince of Texcoco fled from the city after his father was killed and became a fugitive for ten years, hiding in many cities where rulers befriended him.[13]

1426   Tezozomoc, king of Azcapotzalco, died at the age of one hundred and six. The wise tyrant was succeeded by this son Maxtla who proved to be a stupid, cruel ruler. Surrounding nations resented his brutal rule and declared war against him. [14]

[10] Patricia Fent Ross, "Regional Dances of Mexico," *Dance Magazine,* June, 1949, p. 292.

[11] Ibid.

[12] Smith, p. 137.

[13] Fent Ross, p. 293.

[14] Ibid.

1428	The Triple Alliance formed by the three nations Tenochtitlán, Texcoco, and Tacuba, conquered Maxtla of Azcapotzalco. Netzahualcóyotl returned as king of Texcoco. Until the arrival of the Spaniards, Tenochtitlán was a very strong nation, supported by the Mexica and the Azcapotzalco people.[15]
1440	Moctezuma I spread the Aztec domination to Puebla, Veracruz and Morelos.[16]
1469	The king Axayacatl ruled Oaxaca, when the Aztec army was defeated in the west by the Tarascans.[17]
1472	After an illustrious reign, Netzahualcóyotl, poet king of Texcoco, died.[18]
1489	A twin temple, in which thousands were sacrificed, was dedicated to the rain and war gods by the king Ahuitzotl.[19]
1492	Columbus arrived in America. The Spaniards explored the coasts of Central America and the northern coast of South America. They conquered the inhabitants and founded cities.[20]
1502	Moctezuma II was crowned king. His reign was plagued

[15] Fent Ross, p. 293.

[16] Smith, p. 137.

[17] Ibid.

[18] Ibid.

[19] Ibid.

[20] Fent Ross, p. 293.

by a series of bad omens.[21]

1507   The fifty-two year calendrical cycle began, with the celebration of the Fire Ceremony.[22]

1517   Diego Velásquez, governor of Cuba, sent a trading expedition led by Hernández de Cordoba to the coastal area of the Gulf of Mexico.[23]

1518   A second trading expedition was led by Juan de Grijalva. It was the gold obtained from the Indigenous people during this expedition that convinced Spain that Mexico's riches were worth conquering.[24]

1519   (February) Hernán Cortés sailed from Cuba to Yucatán with six hundred men in eleven ships and sixteen horses.[25]

(April) Cortés landed first in Yucatán, then in Tabasco, then in Veracruz where emissaries from Moctezuma brought precious gifts in hopes of deterring the Spaniards.[26]

(August) Cortés began his march inland into Mexico. He first conquered and later made friends and allies of

---

[21] Smith, p. 137.

[22] Ibid.

[23] Fent Ross, p. 293.

[24] Ibid., p.294.

[25] Ibid.

[26] Ibid.

the Tlaxcala people.[27]

(November) Cortés arrived in Tenochtitlán. After the destruction of Moctezuma's statue and idols found in great temple, Cortés erected the Christian Cross.[28]

1520   (June 29) Moctezuma was slain.[29]

(June 30) Cortés fled from his disastrous defeat in Tenochtitlán after the event that became known as the *noche triste*.[30]

1521   (August) Cuahtémoc, the last ruler of the Aztecs, surrendered Tenochtitlán to Cortés and became his prisoner.[31]

1523   The first Franciscan friars landed at Veracruz.[32]

1525   (February) Because of his part in a conspiracy, Cuahtémoc was executed during Cortés's expedition to Honduras.[33]

[27] Ibid.

[28] Stevenson, p. xii.

[29] Ibid.

[30] Ibid.

[31] Ibid.

[32] Ibid.

[33] Ibid.

DEVELOPMENT OF DANCE

Dance was an important part of the religious worship of the Aztecs. Their dances were spiritually symbolic; mysterious beyond understanding; strange and surprising; and almost supernatural in concept. With dance, the Aztecs at first honored heavenly beings: the sun, the moon, and the stars. Dance later honored war gods.[34]

In the Aztec palaces, grand balls took place. It was the social obligation of the nobles to be able to execute dances perfectly. In addition to the responsibility for dance instruction, the priests also conducted dance practices for the ceremonies and balls. All of the people from the king to the members of the lower social class had an opportunity to participate in dance.[35]

Instruction in song and dance was conducted in special buildings constructed particularly for that purpose. These, the *mixcoacalli* or *cuicacalli*, were built close to the ceremonial temples and the palaces of the Aztec nobles and rulers.[36] This indicates that music and dance education was highly significant to these people. In the *mixcoacalli* and *cuicacalli* Aztecs learned tribal tradition and their Náhuatl language as well as song and dance.[37]

In Frederick A. Peterson's *Ancient Mexico*, an old Franciscan manuscript is quoted. It was taken from the Friar/Historian Gerónimo de Mendieta's *historia eclesiastica indiana* and provides a valuable description of the dances of the Aztecs:

> One of the principle artistic expressions in this land was their singing and dancing, executed mainly for solemnizing the festivities of their gods, but also for rejoicing and amusement. In each town and in each nobleman's house, there was a separate build-

[34] Guillermo Jiménez, "The Art of the Dance in Mexico," *The Dancing Times,* August, 1953, p.622.

[35] Peterson, p. 212.

[36] Ibid.

[37] Ibid.

ing with singers and composers of dances and songs. When they had good bass voices they were greatly esteemed, because the nobles in their houses used to sing a great deal in a low pitch.

Ordinarily they sang and danced during their main festivals, held every twenty days. The main dances were held in the town square; other times in the ruler's or noble's patio....

When the dancers arrived at the dance place, the drummers placed themselves in the playing position. The two best singers began the song. The ruler, with the other elders and nobles, walked in front of the drums while singing. They spread out in a circle, three or four arm's length around the drums. The rest of the multitude joined in and made other circles around them. Those who danced in this fashion, in the larger towns, numbered more than a thousand. There were sometimes more than two thousand dancing at once.

Listening to the drums, the people began to dance after they had caught the tempo and the song. The songs began in a low pitch and to a slow beat....

Each verse is repeated three or four times. After a verse ended, the first verse seemed longer because it was set in slower tempo. When the drum muted its tone, all stopped singing. The master singers began another song in a higher tone and livelier beat. Some boys, sons of nobles, seven and eight years old, and even those of four and five, sang in a high voice, they made a pleasing addition to the song.....

Then the songs and dances became livelier, and the sound was so pleasing, that it seemed as if they were singing an old church hymn of gay air. The drums also began to raise their tone, and as the people that were dancing were numerous the sound of the multitude could be heard a long way, especially when quiet air carried the voice, and even more so at night when all was still, and to dance at night they built many great fires and it was certainly a sight to see.[38]

It was clear that dance was an essential element in the Aztec culture. No other element of cultural expression more closely reflects

[38] Ibid., p. 213.

the total experiences of what is Aztec than the Aztec dance, which expresses the intensity of their experiences both emotional and spiritual.[39] "Sacred" dances added solemnity to religious celebrations and "profane" dances added enjoyment to social and domestic festivals. Essentially Aztecs danced for two main purposes: to prepare for war and celebrate its victories or to pay homage to their gods in religious ceremonies.[40]

Dance themes reflected the occasion being celebrated. These could have been the beauty of a sunset, unusual weather phenomena, war victories or defeats, sacrifices to the gods, or domestic activities such as marriages, anniversaries, births, deaths, hunting, fishing, or harvesting.[41] These dance themes can be divided into four categories: religious, which included both sacred and profane dances; historical, which included war and victory dances; natural, which included fertility dances and dances depicting animals or flowers; and recreational, which included spectacular, theatrical dances performed chiefly for entertainment.[42] (The idea for this categorization was suggested to the writer by the classification of Mexican masks used by Donald Cordry in *Mexican Masks.*)

Religious dance themes include sacred or profane dance rituals. Because each god had been invested with a particular character, any trait, skill, or composition which could be attributed to that god's character was dedicated to the god in a sacred dance. Costumes rich with symbols of the particular god were worn by dancers as they imitated the god:

> For example, on the festival of the goddess of the hunt, *Mixcoatl,* they initiated activities of the hunt; those of fishing when they

[39] Dickins, p. 5.

[40] Jiménez, "The Art of Dance in Mexico," p. 621.

[41] Samuel Martí and Gertrude P. Kurath, *Dances of Anáhuac* (Chicago: Aldine Publishing Company, 1964), pp. 38-66.

[42] Donald Cordry, *Mexican Masks* (Texas: University of Texas Press, 1980), pp. 226-245.

feted *Apochtli;* for *Centeotl,* they simulated in pantomime the gathering of fruits and roots, organized a battle of flowers and they adorned themselves with flowers; for *Huitzilipochtli,* the Aztecs mimicked a combat, with the warriors, personages of the court, and the king himself taking part.[43]

Historical dance themes included war and victory dances. The various Indigenous tribes in Mexico honored different war gods. To celebrate war victories, the Aztecs often danced with their captives as they shouted praises to a war god. Auguste Génin in *Notes on the Dances, Music and Songs of the Ancient and Modern Mexicans* states that sometimes the Aztec "conquerors forced the vanquished to dance to exhaustion," and that the victors literally "killed them through dancing."[44] It appears that the dances were also used to torture their prisoners of war. The Opate people from Sonora carried the scalps of the enemies they had killed at war in their festival dances as they celebrated their victories. Like the Aztecs, the Opates also forced all those captured, including women and children, to dance without ceasing. The Opates burned their captives with fiery torches or branding instruments to force them to continue dancing.[45]

Natural dance themes included fertility rites, mimetic dances of animals and flowers, and symbolic dances of the elements of nature. Occasionally, during fertility rite festivals, erotic dances were performed which included phallic rituals and even sexual orgies.[46] The coupling of male and female during religious ritual was believed to create a magic in planting ceremonies during which the deities made the fields fertile.[47]

[43] Auguste Génin, *Notes on the Dances, Music, and Songs of the Ancient and Modern Mexicans,* Annual Report Smithsonian Institution, 1922, p. 659.

[44] Ibid., p. 663.

[45] Ibid., p. 664.

[46] Peterson, p. 214.

[47] Ibid.

Spanish observers, usually priests, wrote partial descriptions of a great number of these erotic dances; however, personal inhibitions and religious convictions prevented these writers from describing dances of this sort in total detail.[48] In many of these descriptions the indignation of the historian observing the erotic dances is very apparent. Father Durán, also quoted by Frederick Peterson in his book *Ancient Mexico*, observed such a dance in apparent disapproval:

> There was a dance so provocative and indecent, in which the people wiggle so much and make such faces and engage in so much indecent flirtation, that it seems to be a dance for loose women and men of doubtful habits, and they called it *cuecuecheuyacatl,* which means wriggling, scratching, or itchy dance.[49]

Martí and Kurath in *Dances of Anáhuac* tell of the fecundation rite called *motzontecomaitótia*, a ceremony in which a person was sacrificed. Later, it became a ceremony where live roosters or turkey cocks are hung from ropes. Men on horseback gallop by, catch the cocks, wring their necks, and behead them. In Mexico today, magical rites of this sort called *costumbres* are still performed in the guise of a sport.[50]

Many natural dances included mimicking of all kinds of animals and plants. Génin recounts an interesting description of the festival of the birds:

> ...men and women dressed like birds, danced and whistled while turning, leaped unto the trees, threw themselves into the water as simulating aquatic birds, or threw themselves on the grass; imitating in every which way the birds whose plumage they wore or which they pretended to represent. [51]

[48] Ibid.

[49] Ibid.

[50] Martí and Kurath, pp. 52-56.

[51] Génin, p.665.

In mimicking animals or plants, the dancers wore costumes made of the actual skins of animals or the plumage of birds, or they donned leaves, fruits, or flowers of the plants they represented.[52]

Recreational dance themes included theatrical spectacles performed chiefly for entertainment. Both conquerors and the Spanish nobility admired the gymnastic and acrobatic feats of the Aztecs. This type of dance was a graceful spectacle requiring strength and braveness. In his *History of Mexico*, Hubert Bancroft vividly describes a feat similar to the famous "Chinese foot-balancing trick in which the performers lying on his back, spins a heavy pole on the soles of his raised feet, throws it up, catches it, and twirls it in every direction."[53] Another athletic stunt is described by Bancroft:

> A favorite feat was for three men, mounted one on the shoulders of another, and the third standing on the head of the second, to move slowly around the circle of spectators, while a kind of dance was performed by the man at the top of a beam, the lower end of which was forked, and rested on the shoulders of two other dancers...Some raised a stick from the ground, with a man balanced at the end of it; others leaped upon a stick set upright in the ground, or danced upon the tight-rope.[54]

Humorous dances were included in the Aztec repertoire of recreational dances. In some, the dancers donned masks and wore humps like hunchbacks to provoke laughter from the audience. In others, buffoons would appear, mimicking the people of other tribes by making funny faces and engaging in verbal ridicule.[55] On festival days these burlesque spectacles were a favorite means of entertain-

---

[52] Ibid., pp. 665-666.

[53] Hubert Howe Bancroft, *History of Mexico* (New York: The Bancroft Company, 1914), p.82.

[54] Ibid., p. 82.

[55] Génin, p. 659.

ment for the Aztecs after dinner. The deaf, lame, blind, sick, and deformed were ridiculed. Sometimes even prominent citizens, merchants, and mechanics were mimicked.[56]

Single formations were often utilized in Aztec dances. In the ceremonial and ritual dances, performers formed circles, concentric circles, straight lines, or serpentine designs. Large concentric circles were the most widely used dance formations in communal celebrations. Patterns of advance, withdrawal, and exchange of place were performed in the single and double file formations. The musicians with their sacred drums, the *teponaztli* and *huehuetl,* were always centered in the circular formations formed by the nobility and the populace.[57]

Although women were involved in some dances, only males customarily took part in the ritual dances. When the two sexes danced together, there was no bodily contact.[58] According to historian Patricia Fent Ross, in religious communal dance, Aztecs of both sexes took part. In her article, "Regional Dances of Mexico," Fent Ross describes this ancient dance as a "wheel dance:"

> The musicians formed the hub, with the most important men of the tribe in the inner circle; the older men and women formed the next circle; the younger people the next circle; and the children danced in the outermost circle. All the participants held fixed arm and body positions in relation to the imaginary wheel spokes. While the inner circle danced almost vertically in circling the musicians, the outermost circle was practically running to keep the wheel perfect.[59]

In the same article Fent Ross gives evidence of a non-ritualistic

[56] Bancroft, p. 81.

[57] Peterson, p. 212.

[58] Génin, p. 659.

[59] Patricia Fent Ross, "Regional Dances of Mexico," *Dance Magazine,* June, 1949, p. 13.

couple dance which was performed at private social festivities. In this dance, the men and women "formed two lines, much in the same manner as the minuet, dancing as a unit, with the lines intermingling. The line dancers would mark time in place while a single couple performed improvising steps to the music" between the lines.[60]

In terms of costume, there were differences among the classes. Luxurious clothing was normally worn by the nobility at these ceremonies. In contrast, "the common men disguised themselves as animals, wearing costumes consisting of animal skins, feathers, and leather or wooden masks" to conceal their faces.[61]

Juan de Torquemada's description of the costume is reproduced in Hubert Bancroft's *History of Mexico* which states,

> ...All appeared at the dances as richly attired as their means would permit. Noted warriors appeared magnificently dressed, and sometimes wore shields adorned with feathers. Nobles wore a courtly dress with the outer garment being a rich mantle knotted at the shoulder...In their hair were tassels of feathers and gold. In their lips were ornaments of gold and precious stones. In their ears were golden rings. Around their wrists were bracelets of the same metal and strings of turquoises. Some had gold bells attached to their ankles...The gaily colored garments of the lower classes were decorated with feathers and embroidery; garlands encircled the head; about the neck were strings of shells and beans; and on the arms and necks were bracelets. The women were attired in gaily colored dresses, fancifully embroidered, and adorned with fringe.[62]

In their early ceremonial dances, the Aztecs frequently employed masks in order to endow the dancers with a reality suggest-

[60] Ibid., p.12.

[61] Guillermo Jiménez, *danzas de méxico* (México: Colección Anáhuac de Arte Mexicano, 1948), p.6.

[62] Bancroft, p. 80.

ing birds, wild beasts, snakes, or gods.[63] Occasionally, the face of the dancer was painted. The historian, Guillermo Jiménez, in his book *Danzas de México,* describes the surrealistic effect produced by a masked dancer:

> The mask miraculously perpetuates a gesture or it aroused in the eager spirit of the spectator a perfect emotion. The turns, movements, steps of a masked performer are fixed in the mind with greater plasticity, greater solemnity, enveloped in a realm of mystery.[64]

Aztec music was predominately percussive. Percussive instruments were customarily used for dance accompaniment. These included drums with a fixed or a variable pitch; the *teponaztli* (a kind of xylophone); the *huehuetl* (a slit-drum); the *tlapanhuehuetl,* a drum which was worn suspended around the neck; *conchas* (*seashells*)*;* wood horns or trumpets; whistles, fluters, or *chirimias* (fifes); "oboes" made of reed, wood, bone, or clay; rasping instruments made of animal bones; bells, *sonajas* (rattles), and shakers made of gourds, wood, or cast metal.[65] Musical composition and dance choreography depended on sharp changes of rhythm to provide variety and effect.

As might be expected the music and dance preferred by the young and the old differed. The stately dance style of the noble lords contrasted drastically with the livelier songs and more rapid dance meters preferred by the young people.[66]

In the sections which follow, two types of Aztec dances are described: the *Mecavaliztli,* meaning sacred dances, and the *Metotiliztli,* meaning secular or profane dances.[67]

---

[63] Jiménez, "The Art of the Dance in Mexico," p. 622.

[64] Jiménez, *danzas de méxico, p.6.*

[65] Zabre, p. 92.

[66] Ibid., p. 93.

[67] Jiménez, *danzas de méxico, p. 6.*

Mecavaliztli: Sacred Ceremonial Dances

The Aztecs measured time by using three overlapping calendars. The three calendars were the sacred calendar, the calendar of omens, and the solar calendar.[68] These calendars divided the year into eighteen months of twenty days each, with five days, known as *nenomtemi,* left over to even out the year. Each day in the Aztec calendar was represented by "its god or goddess, its legend, and its distinguishing emblem."[69] Every season had its festival, and every festival had its own ceremonial dance.[70]

There were eighteen ceremonies based on the eighteen months of the solar calendar. Half of these were celebrated with dance:

1. Fourth month, *Uei Tozoztli,* honors the god *Chicomecoatl* and other agrarian gods. Flowers and food were offered to the gods, and ceremonial rites included girls singing in procession and dancing.[71]
2. Fifth month, *Toxcatl,* honors the god *Huitzilopochtil,* the Aztec solider deity.[72] Young men who had been treated as royalty for a year in preparation were sacrificed.[73] In the ceremonies, men danced the serpent dance, women performed a leaping dance, and young girls performed the "popcorn dance."[74]

[68] Pierre and Janine Soissen, *Life of the Aztecs in Ancient Mexico,* trans. David Macrae (Spain: Editions Minerva, S.A., 1978), p.114.

[69] Génin, p. 663.

[70] Covarrubias, p.1.

[71] Soisson, p. 115.

[72] Martí and Kurath, pp. 38-42.

[73] Soisson, p. 115.

[74] Martí and Kurath, pp. 38-42.

3. Seventh month, *Tecuilhuitontli,* honors the goddess of salt and salt water, *Huixtocihuatl.* A woman personifying the goddess was sacrificed.[75] Before being sacrificed, the woman wrapped in an ocelot skin and wearing golden bells or *sonajas* (rattles) performed a fertility dance.[76]

4. Eighth month, *Uei Tecuilhuitl,* honors *Xilonen,* the goddess who protected the new corn.[77] After an all-night song vigil and purification with incense, a woman, whose face was painted in two different colors and who represented the goddess, was put to death. The ceremonial dance was performed by women bedecked in flower garlands. Men performed the "serpent dance."[78]

5. Ninth month, *Tlaxochimaco,* honors *Huitzilopochtli* or *Xochilhuitl.*[79] All kinds of flowers were used to decorate his temple. There was a huge festivity, where during a banquet, much singing and dancing took place.[80]

6. Tenth month, *Xocotl Huetzi,* honors *Xiuhtecuhtli,* the god of fire. Prisoners of war were decapitated in sacrifice to this god. As part of the ceremonial rites, young people climbed a greased pole topped with a paste effigy of the god in order to retrieve a piece of the effigy.[81] In ceremonial dances, Aztecs danced in pairs with the war captives in serpent like motions.[82]

---

[75] Ibid., pp. 47-50.

[76] Martí and Kurtath, p.42.

[77] Soisson, p. 115.

[78] Martí and Kurath, p. 42.

[79] Ibid., pp. 47-50.

[80] Soisson, p.115.

[81] Ibid.

[82] Martí and Kurath, pp. 51-52.

7. Eleventh month, *Ochpaniztli,* honors the terrestrial gods who "swept" the way of the gods. "A woman was sacrificed to the Lady of the Serpents, Mother-Earth" (*Coalticue*), and the king reviewed his warriors.[83] Ceremonial dances included the "serpent dance" and the "hand waving" dance.[84]
8. Fourteenth month, *Quecholli,* honors *Mixcoatl,* the god of the hunt. Entrusting their children to the old priestesses, the mothers would watch while the priestesses first embraced the children and then had them dance.[85]
9. Seventeenth month, *Tititl,* honors *Llamatecuhtli,* "Ancient Lady" or "Mother-Earth."[86] "A woman clad in white, personifying the goddess, was put to death..."[87] For the ceremonial rites "a grotesque battle" with a carnival-like atmosphere was organized where young women were chased through the streets by young men who hit them with pillows all the way.[88]

In many ceremonial dances, performers imitated animal movements in fertility rites. [89]

Throughout the year in ceremonial dances, the Aztecs honored a large diversity of gods.[90] The main purpose of the sacred ceremonial dances was to entreat these gods to grant specific requests. In essence, they dedicated to each god their daily occupation, every event

---

[83] Soisson, p.115.

[84] Martí and Kurath, pp. 51-52.

[85] Soisson, p. 116.

[86] Martí and Kurath, p. 52-56.

[87] Soisson, p.116.

[88] Ibid.

[89] Génin, p. 665.

[90] Peterson, pp. 202-203.

which occurred on that date, or simply celebrated everything which recalled the functions, attributes, or character of the god.[91] For the Aztecs, the god's behavior reflected the totality of men's accomplishments and failings. Both by imitation and symbolism, the Aztec dances honored these gods who represented aspects of the life of both mortals and immortals.[92]

In the minds of the Aztecs, an individual's relationship with deities took precedence over one's relationship with other individuals. Expression of these relationships were represented through dance.[93]The historian Durán indicates that the dance honoring the war-god, *Huizilopochtli*, was the Aztecs' favorite. In Dickins, *Dances of Mexico*, this description of the dance effectively conveys its sense of beauty:

> In an arbour of roses in the temple of the god, sat a woman, representing *Xochiquetzalli*, the goddess of beauty, love and flowers, surrounded by dancers adorned with roses. In nearby artificial trees, filled with fragrant roses, little boys dressed brilliantly as birds and butterflies, jumped from branch to branch, sipping the nectar of the flowers. When the men, dressed as gods, came out of the temple and pretended to kill the birds, *Xochiquetzalli* appeared and led the men into her rose arbour, seating them near her and according them the respect and honour due to the gods, they represented.[94]

In her book, *Mexican Folkways*, Frances Toor describes another ceremonial Aztec dance honoring the gods *Macuilxochitl* (five flower) and *Xochipilli* (god of dance, music, and song):

> The fiesta in his honor, on a movable date, was called *Xochi-*

---

[91] Génin, p. 663.

[92] Ibid., p. 663.

[93] Jiménez, "The Art of Dance in Mexico," p. 622.

[94] Dickins, pp. 5-6.

Ihuitl, the fiesta of the flowers. For four days before it took place the people fasted, and if husbands and wives slept together, they would be afflicted with a serious disease. On the day of the fiesta a man was dressed in the adornments of his god, as if he were his image. With him the worshippers sang, danced, and played the *teponaztli.* At noon many quail were beheaded, their blood was spilled before the god, and the people offered him blood from their ears and tongues, pierced with maguey needles. Various offerings were made in the form of food—toasted corn, tamales, arrow, and figures of corn dough.[95]

The most important deity in the Aztec culture was *Quetzalcóatl.* Every eight years the solar cycle and the heliac hortus of Venus fell on the same date at which time Venus and the sun were both visible in the sky. According to legend, the celebration of this occasion had so much significance that the Aztecs believed that the god *Quetzalcóatl* participated with them during this celebration.[96]

The *Atamalqualiztli* (the eating of water tamales made without salt, pepper, lime, or chili) was the festival celebrating the eight year cycle. On this occasion, honoring *Quetzalcóatl,* merchants retired to the Aztec temples, while, in the grand courtyard, the people rejoiced with dancing and comedies.[97] Some participants costumed themselves as "birds, butterflies, frogs, and beetles; and others pretended to be lame, armless, and crippled, the feast coming to an end with dancing."[98]

La Danza del Volador (Dance of the Flyers), one of the oldest surviving Mexican Pre-Hispanic dances, may have come from the Huaxteca-Totonac region as part of a spectacular religious rite in which a sacrificial victim perished by bow and arrow.[99] In Frederick

[95] Toor, p. 299.

[96] Martí and Kurath, p.59.

[97] Ibid.

[98] Zabre, p.93.

[99] Covarrubias, p.4.

Peterson's *Ancient Mexico*, a detailed description of *La Danza de los Voladores* is given:

> A pole one hundred feet tall was erected, with a movable platform fitted over the top. Four ropes are attached to the platform and wound around the pole. Five men, representing the five directions of the earth, [and] who were once dressed as birds, climbed up the pole by the ropes. The captain stands in the center of the tiny platform, which is not more than fourteen inches in diameter, and plays a tiny drum with one hand and a small flute with the other. To make matters more exciting he dances on top of the pole and whirls around.

> At the bottom of the pole several musicians play a *chirimia* (flute) and drums. The other four men, on top of the pole, seat themselves on cross poles which are hung by ropes from the four sides of the platform and tie the loose ends of the four ropes around their waists. Then they raise their feet and throw themselves backward off the poles. The captain stays on the platform while it revolves. The ropes around the pole are so arranged that the platform turns around thirteen times before the men reach the ground. The men move their arms as they fly through the air to imitate the birds of the world directions [sic], and to symbolize the passage of time. The entire dance seems to symbolize the fifty-two year religious cycle of the Mexican calendar (multiplying thirteen turns by four ropes).[100]

The religious significance of this dance long ago disappeared, but *La Danza del Volador* still survives. It is performed by the Totonac, Otomí, and Huaxteca people for Christian festivals such as the feast of Corpus Christi in Papantla, Veracruz and at other festivals.[101] It still requires unusual skill and agility; it still typifies the spirit and emotion, the color and pageantry, and especially the "strength and courage of the people" who are of Indigenous descent.

[100]Peterson, pp. 205-206.

[101] Covarrubias, p. 4.

Metotiliztli: Secular Ceremonial Dances

Information regarding the precise character of secular ceremonial dances is meager; however, the early chronicles give descriptions of collective dances. A number of these secular ceremonial dances have been recorded by Bernardino de Sahagún, Francisco López de Gómara, Francisco Hernández, Juan de Torquemada, Bernal Díaz, Antonio Herrera, Francisco Cervantes de Salazár and Father Pedro Acosta. Recorded accounts give different views of the dances.

Aztec rituals were not all bloody and gruesome. As Fray Bernardino de Sahagún observed, "There was much beauty and perfection presented by highly trained and picturesque costumed dancers. There were dancers in connection with all elaborate temple services."[102]

Bernardino de Sahagún, in Robert Stevenson's *Music in Mexico*, comments on the conscientious preparation for the feasts and dances by the Lords:

One thing that the Chiefs took great pains with were the *areitos*, the dances which were festivals for the entire people. The leader of the singing first gave his instructions to the singers in his charge, and told them how to pitch their voices and tune them; the leader also told them what kind of *ule* (rubber) sticks they were to use in playing the *teponaztli*. He also gave orders for the steps and postures that were to be used in dancing...[103]

The dance hall in which these secular festivals took place, the *Mixcoacalli*, is described by Sahagún in Martí and Kurath's *Dances of Anáhuac:*

There was a hall, which was called *Mixcoacalli*. In this place the singers of Mexico and Tlatilulco met to await the commands of

[102] Irna Fergusson, *Fiesta in Mexico.* (New York: Alfred A. Knopf, Inc., 1934), pp. 8-9.

[103] Robert Murrell Stevenson, *Music in Mexico: A Historical Survey* (New York: Thomas Y. Crowell Company, 1954), p. 25.

the Principal [in case] he wished to [have them] dance, rehearse, or hear the newly composed songs. They had at hand all the vestments for the dances (*areito*); drum (*huehuetl*); slit-drum (*teponaztli*), with the accessories, to play them and some rattles called *ayacachtli*, and *tetzilácatl* (gong) and a *omichicahuaztli* (bone notched stick); and also several flutes:

[There were present] all the master musicians, singers, dancers, and the costumes for the dances of any hymn or chant. If the Principal commanded that they sing [and dance] the chants of *Uexotzincáyotl* or *Anahuacáyotl*, and if the Principal ordered that the masters (musicians and dancers) and the singers perform and dance the chant which is called *Cuextecáyotl*, they put on the vestments of these dances, according to the chant. [They] made themselves up with wigs and painted masks with perforated noses (holes in the nose in order to breathe) and bright reddish hair wigs. They carried (gave the impression of) a longish broad head, as is common with the *Cuextecas*, and they put on woven capes, like nets. Thus, the singers, [dancers, musicians] had many and various costumes for any ballet (*areito* or series of dances) and for the chants and each dance.[104]

Francisco López de Gómara was Cortés's personal chaplain after 1540. The following is a festival dance description by him, quoted by Robert Murrell Stevenson in *Music in Mexico*:

The two drums (*teponaztli* and *huehuetl*) were played in unison with the striking chants. The performers sang merry, joyful, and amusing tunes or some ballads in praise of past kings, recounting their wars of life events.

When it was time to begin, eight or ten men lustily blew their whistles. The drums were beaten lightly. The dancers appeared in rich white, red, green, and yellow garments interwoven with various different colors. In their hands they carried bouquets of roses, feathered fans, gold and feathered headdresses, while many of them appeared with garlands of scented flowers. Many wore fitted feather-work hoods covering the head

---

[104] Martí and Kurath, pp. 60-62.

and shoulders, or else masks were worn to represent an eagle, a tiger, an alligator, or wild animal heads. Thousands of dancers assembled to perform. There were leading men, nobles, and even lords. The higher the man's rank, the closer was his position with respect to the drums... They played, sang, danced quietly in a solemn nature, but as they became more excited, they sang carols and jolly tunes. As the dance became livelier, the movements and music changed tempo.[105]

The Aztecs utilized various styles and forms of dancing during a festival. One particular form was called the *netotiliztil,* meaning *areito.* The *areitos* (songs and series of dances associated with a ceremony or festival) were composed at the same time by the poet-musician. As Dr. Francisco Hernández, a special envoy of Philip II of Spain pointed out, the unity of the people in performing these *areitos* (ballets) was remarkable, especially when three or four thousand people at the large celebrations memorized the variations in movement for every individual song.[106] This was also true for dramatic productions in which all of the people participated.

The description of the *netotiliztli* by the sixteenth century Franciscan-historian Juan de Torquemada, paints a lively picture of the exciting festival. The dances and music reflected the mood of the celebration, which was joyous and pleasure-seeking. Torquemada described the festival of *netotiliztli* as a circus-pageant, the purpose of which was to entertain important emissaries, the Principals, or just the people themselves. Many people took part, including musicians, dancers, actors, acrobats, readers of poetry, clown, and dwarfs. Others danced on stilts, and there was "a man who danced holding two men on his shoulders who carried bouquets of flowers and plumes in their hands."[107]

The eighteen century Jesuit-historian Francisco Clavigero recorded a similar version of the dance described by Juan de Torque-

[105] Stevenson, p.26.

[106] Martí and Kurath, pp. 62-63.

[107] Ibid., p.63.

mada. He called this communal dance the *neteteliztli*. A written description of this dance in the Spanish language was found in *la breve historia de la música en México* by Guillermo Velásquez but the same version written in the English language can be found in *History of Mexico*, written by Hubert Bancroft. His version of the *neteteliztli* states:

> ... At a given signal set by the musicians, the dance leaders initiated the movements as the entire company imitated the movements of the feet, arms, heads, and bodies in perfect unison. The dancers kept the perfect timing with their rattles.
>
> ...The motions varied throughout the dance. With either the right side or left side partner, the dancers either held hands or held each other by the waist.
>
> ...After the first song, usually in honor of the gods, kings, and heroes stating the events of the day, a popular ode was sung in a higher scale and to a livelier measure. Flutes, trumpets, and whistles were used to increase the effect.
>
> ... Each song lasted an hour, while the dances were performed continuously. As dancers became tired, they were replaced by another set of dancers throughout the entire day. Meanwhile, jesters and clowns intermingled between the line of dancers, uttering jokes, cutting capers, and serving refreshments.[108]

In reference to this type of entertainment Bernal Díaz states that Moctezuma II engaged many dancers and buffoons during his monarchy. These dancers performed in novel ways, on stilts or flying like birds around a tree as they danced. Their purpose was to entertain the king. [109]

Entertainment was not the only purpose fulfilled by dance. Dance expressed many distinctly differing emotions from buffoonery to solemnity. The *mitote*, a sorrowful song-dance synonymous with *areito*, was performed at large communal celebrations. The solemn

[108] Bancroft, p. 80.

[109] Martí and Kurath, p.63.

mitote was considered so noble and honorable that the Aztec king himself often took part. A description of the *mitote* written by Father Pedro Acosta and Francisco Cervantes de Salazár is quoted in *Dances of Anáhuac*:

> In these dances (*mitotes*) they were formed in two circles. The oldsters, Principals and more important people danced in the middle, where the instruments stood. Since they carried pennants in their hands, they hardly moved while they danced and sang. The heads and bodies of the dancers were bent forward as they sang these sorrowful songs. The others, arranged in pairs, formed another wide and spacious circle as they danced together taking faster steps and leaping movements.[110]

In *Dances of Anáhuac,* Antonio Herrera is quoted with this description of the solemn *mitote*, the *Netecuitotilo* (Lordly Dance):

> That night more than one thousand knights got together in the temple with great loud sounds of drums, shell-trumpets, coronets (flutes) and notched bones. They whistled loudly and sang many hymns. They danced nude, with only their secret parts covered and with headdresses of colorful feathers, jewels, gold necklaces, and ribbons around their bodies. Some wore armlets, bracelets and plates of gold on their chests and backs. They danced in the courtyard of the temple in the presence of the Spanish, a dance whose name means merit with work, *mereci-miento con trabajo*. Their songs were of pious character and with them they begged for water, bread, health, victory, peace and sons. They danced in a circle holding their hands, in rows and keeping time to the tune of the musicians and singers.[111]

Curt Sachs in *World History of Dance* lists some of the noble participants in the *Netecuitotilo* (Lordly Dance):

[110] Ibid., p. 65.

[111] Ibid. p. 63.

They form on the outside; Motecuhcoma [Moctezuma] leading the dance, comes followed by the others; the two great kings, Nacaualpilli, King of Tetzcoco, and Totoquiuaztli, King of Tepaneca, come up to his side; the spectators are gripped with fear as the dance proceeds.[112]

The *Netecuitotilo* (Lordly Dance) can be classified as both religious and a secular ceremonial dance. It was performed at celebrations held at the beginning of new solar cycles, once every four years. Because the Aztec war god *Huitzilopochtli* was associated with the sun, this dance helped celebrate not only the solar cycle but also the war god's connection with the sun and its cycles. The *Netecuitotilo* was magnificently performed by Aztec nobility, the chiefs and the Jaguar and Eagle Knight Warriors.[113]

Having observed many performances of religious and secular dances in Mexico City; Monterrey, Nuevo León; Nuevo Laredo, Tamaulipas; and in various cities in Texas such as Austin, San Antonio, and Laredo; I can draw comparisons between dances described in the literature and dances observed in my lifetime. Many of the Indigenous dance movements, themes, and movement patterns in religious and secular dances are still performed today. Churchyards, auditoriums, and dance concert halls, have replaced the temple square; dancers ornament themselves with tin, glass, and feathers instead of precious stones, gold, and silver; sandals of soft deer-skin embroidered with gold many now be rough, heavy-soled boots or *huaraches* (leather sandals), but the sense of line, color, precision, discipline, style of movement, and the devotion that animated their ancestors are ever present.

[112] Curt Sachs, *World History of Dance* (New York: WW. Norton and Company, Inc., 1937), p. 142

[113] Martí and Kurath, p.56.

Sanjuanita Martínez-Hunter gives a presentation on Mexican Dance History during the late 1970s at the University of Texas at Austin as pictured above. Pictured below: Sanjuanita Martínez-Hunter speaks to her students of the UT Ballet Folklorico right before a performance in the late 1970s. Photos courtesy of the Sanjuanita Martínez-Hunter Collection.

CHAPTER 2: DANCE IN MEXICO (1519-1525) - THE SPANISH INFLUENCE AFTER THE CONQUEST

The period examined in this chapter consists of two stages: discovery and conquest. The period of exploration and discovery of Mexico started in 1492 with the first voyage of Columbus and extended through 1519 with the expedition of Cortés. There were, however, direct consequences of the latter which lasted until the year 1525.[1]

The exploration and conquest of Mexico actually began in 1517. The process was directed from Cuba by Governor Diego Velásquez who sent a total of three expeditions to the Mexican mainland. Francisco Hernández de Córdoba led the first expedition in 1517, Juan de Grijalva led the second one the following year, and Hernán Cortés led the expedition in 1519.[2] During his stops in Yucatán and Tabasco, Cortés met Jerónimo de Aguilar; he also acquired an Indigenous slave girl, La Malinche, who was later christened Marina. These two individuals greatly assisted Cortés as interpreters.[3]

In Aztec legend, there is a belief that the plumed "White God" *Quetzalcóatl,* would return to rule his people. Thus, scholars believed that when Cortés came to Mexico in his ship powered by white sun-bleached sails, the Aztecs mistook him for *Quetzalcóatl.*[4] However, recent scholarship by Mathew Restall in *When Montezuma Met Cortés: the True Story of the Meeting that Changed History* (2018) debunks this myth arguing that this idea of Cortés as mistaken as *Quet-*

[1] Zabre, p. 137.

[2] *Collier's Encyclopedia,* XVI (1981), S.v. "Mexico."

[3] Meyer, p. 102.

[4] Ibid., p.106.

zalcóatl, is purely fiction having been invented by the Spanish chroniclers to justify the conquest.[5]

Upon arriving to Veracruz in 1519, Cortés and his expedition traveled along the coast of Yucatán and made their way to San Juan de Ulua. Here, Cortés met with Moctezuma's representatives and the Totonac people. He made allies with the Totonac people and left behind a base with a part of his military force. Then, he continued on his journey. On August 20, 1519, Cortés entered the land inhabited by the Tlaxcala people. At first, they fought against him but eventually they became allies. Cortés established a base in this territory and continued onward alongside about one thousand Tlaxcalan troops that accompanied him.[6] Next, Cortés decided to travel to Tenochtitlán by passing through the city of Cholula. The people of this city were allies with the Aztecs. Upon arrival, Cortés' expedition camped outside the city. The Spaniards entered the city and stayed for a few days. After a while, Malinche heard rumors of an up-coming ambush planned against the Spaniards. Cortés summoned all the nobles of Cholula who were unarmed before a great pyramid. They did not deny the rumors. Cortés and his men massacred the nobles. In addition, his expedition attacked the entire city. After pillaging the city of Cholula and massacring its people. The expedition continued onward towards Tenochtitlán.[7]

Cortés and his expedition arrived at Tenochtitlán on November 8. Shortly after their arrival they planned an overthrow capturing

---

[5] Mathew Restall, *When Montezuma Met Cortéz the True Story of the Meeting that Changed History.* (New York: Harper Collins Publishers, 2018), p. 43-35.

[6] Douglas A. Daniel, "Tactical Factors in the Spanish Conquest of the Aztecs," *Anthropological Quarterly,* 65.4 (1992), pp. 187-188.

[7] Geoffrey T. McCafferty, "The Cholula Massacre: Factional Histories and Archeology of the Spanish Conquest," in *The Entangled Past: Integrating History and Archeology,* eds. M. Boyd, J.C. Erwin, and M. Hendrickson (Canada: Proceedings at the Thirtieth Annual Chacmool Conference, 2000), 347-359.

Moctezuma and punishing Aztec commanders. The expedition took siege of the city. However, Cortés left Tenochtitlán to deal with a competing expedition that arrived in Mexico that was sent by the Governor of Cuba. Pedro de Alvarado, a Captain, was in command in his absence.[8] Under his leadership, the Spanish would commit another atrocity resembling the massacre of Cholula: the bloody seizure of Tenochtitlán at dawn on July 1, 1520. This incident is remembered as *la noche triste* (the sad night) and during this sorrowful event, Emperor Moctezuma was killed.[9]

On the night before the massacre, the nobles of Tenochtitlán approached Alvarado to ask permission to celebrate their fiesta of *Toxcatl*.[10] It was the *Netecuitotilo* dance, during the *Toxcatl* fiesta in honor of *Huitzilopochtli*, which the Aztecs wanted to perform.[11] Alvarado consented on the condition that there was to be no human sacrifice. [12]Moctezuma himself led his lavishly clad nobles in the *Netecuitotilo* on the night now known as *la noche triste*.[13]

During the dancing and singing, Alvarado heard a rumor that the ceremonial dances were no more than war dances, ceremonies offered to the Aztec war god in preparation for an attack on the Spanish forces. Alvarado's unfounded report made him believe that the only humans to be sacrificed were the Spaniards. Convinced that this information was accurate and determined to strike the first blow, Captain Alvarado lay siege against the Indigenous people finding them unarmed and without an escape route. The Spanish forces dismembered two hundred Indigenous nobles. As Cortés' forces captured the palace, the Aztecs, stunned and grief stricken, violently re-

[8] Daniel, p.188.

[9] Ibid., p. 122.

[10] Ibid., p. 120.

[11] Martí and Kurath, p. 56.

[12] Daniel, p. 120

[13] Martí and Kurath, p. 56.

taliated.[14]

Following battles with the Aztecs, the Spanish withdrew from Tenochtitlán. They faced heavy casualties. However, Cortés and his allies would later return to defeat the Aztecs in battle at Otumba on July 14, 1520. With reinforcements and supplies the Spanish and their allies held a ninety day siege over Tenochtitlán. They conquered the city on August 13, 1521.[15] Cuauhtémoc, meaning "Falling Eagle" or "Setting Sun," was the last great warrior and ruler of Tenochtitlán when it fell on August 21, 1521.[16] The fall of Tenochtitlán marked the Spanish victory over the Aztec empire.

The Spanish conquistadors set out to conquer the world for God and for their nation. Every expedition carried both the Spanish flag and the Catholic crucifix. The mission was twofold: to expand the borders of Spain and to Christianize any inhabitants. To commemorate a Spanish occupation, the cross and the flag were raised. The priests' foremost mission was to convert and baptize the conquered peoples. In Mexico, the priests found Indigenous people engaged in elaborate religious rites, worshipping many gods and goddesses.[17] Every aspect of the Aztec society was deeply entrenched in religion. After the Spanish Conquest, virtually all forms of cultural expression—music, poetry, dance, drama—were dominated by the Church.[18]

In order to provide a comprehensive overview of the panorama of events occurring during and following the Spanish Conquest of Mexico, Table Two presents a chronological summary. This is followed by a discussion relating the overall historical situation to the development of dance in Mexico.

[14] Ibid., p. 120

[15] Ibid.

[16] *The World Book Encyclopedia*, XI (1956), S.v. "Mexico," by R. Red.

[17] Fergusson, pp. 6-7.

[18] Zabre, p. 151.

Table Two
Historical Chronology

1519   (February) The embarkation of Hernán Cortés to Yucatán, from Cuba consisted of eleven ships, six hundred men, and sixteen horses.[19]

1519   (April) Following interim landings in Yucatán and Tabasco, Cortés and his force landed in a sandy beach, today known as the town of Veracruz.[20]

1519   (August) Cortés led his force into the interior of Mexico, first conquering then befriending and allying with the Indigenous people of Tlaxcala.[21]

1520   (January) Cortés arrived at Tenochtitlán with his force of Spanish soldiers plus some five thousand Tlaxcalan allies. They were received amicably by Moctezuma, who sent them gifts, in hopes they would return to their home.[22]

        (June) The people of Tenochtitlán made an attempt to expel the Spaniards from their city. Following a lengthy siege of the great palace they had inhabited, the Spaniards escaped under cover at night. Cortés lost two-thirds of his men, plus his entire armament of heavy guns. The date June 20, 1520, has been immortalized as *la noche triste*. During the siege, the Emperor Mocte-

---

[19] Fent Ross, *Made in Mexico,* p. 294.

[20] Ibid.

[21] Ibid.

[22] Ibid.

zuma was stoned to death by his own people. [23]

1521	(June) Cortés returned with his reinforced army plus several thousand Indigenous allies to seize the city of Tenochtitlán.[24]
	(August) Cortés conquered the city of Tenochtitlán. The Aztec ruler Cuauhtémoc, who succeeded Moctezuma, surrendered the city to Cortés.[25]
1522	Spanish rules were imposed upon the Tarascans of Michoacán, Central Mexican tribes, and numerous Mixtecs and Zapotecs in Oaxaca.[26]
1524	The arrival of twelve Franciscan monks to Mexico City was welcomed by Cortés. The School of Arts and Crafts for Indian Youths was founded by Pedro de Gante, a relative of Carlos V., King of Spain.[27]
1525	The Spaniards hung Cuauhtémoc, Tenochtiltán's captured ruler, in the Mayan province of Acalán, under the pretext that he was plotting a rebellion. The Aztec Empire came to an end.

[23] Ibid.

[24] Ibid.

[25] Ibid.

[26] Ibid., p. 295.

[27] Smith, p. 169.

DEVELOPMENT OF DANCE

The Spanish conquistadors came to forcefully impose their way of life and morality on the Aztec people. The conquerors saw no value in the Indigenous culture or religion. The Spaniards expelled the Aztec priests from their sacrificial altars, covering the blood stains from human victims with white linen cloths and sanctifying them with Christian crucifixes. [28]

However, the Spanish conquerors faced the problem that many thousands of their Indigenous subjects worshipped through dance. Desiring at all cost to save the souls of the newly conquered people, the conquistadors incorporated polytheistic festivities and dance into their sacramental rites. In their eyes, substituting the symbols and deity of Christianity for the polytheistic motifs and deities while preserving the pomp and color of polytheistic ceremonies helped actualize the transition from the sinful life of certain damnation to the holy life of eternal joy.[29]

As the acculturation progressed, the religious fiestas changed in form. Ancient deities who had presided over the festive rituals were replaced by the patron saints of Christianity. Heroes such as St. James, an Apostle of Christ who appeared in a vision predicting military victory for the Christians over the Moors in the Battle of Clavijo in 844 A.D.[30] and Charlemagne, (742 A.D- 814 A.D.) a Frankish King who militarily conquered Germany, Italy, and Spain and was known as the defender of the Catholic Faith,[31] were introduced in the ceremonial dances. Dance included themes such as the struggle between

[28] Anne Schley Duggan, et.al., *Folk Dances of the United States and Mexico* (New York: A.S. Barnes and Company, 1948), p. 103.

[29] Ibid.

[30] John A. Crow, *Spain: The Root and the Flower; an Interpretation of Spain and the Spanish People* (Berkeley: University of California Press, 2005), p. 84.

[31] Richard Winston, *Charlemagne* (New York: American Heritage Publishing, 2016), pp. 6-8.

Christianity and atheism, the medieval Crusades, and even the Spanish Conquest.[32]

Because the Spaniards believed that all the symbolism of a dance was dictated by the theme, they allowed the Indigenous people to continue their dances. The patronizing Spaniards, underestimated the sophistication of the Aztec dances, oversimplifying their motions to mere technical skill and graceful acrobatics as, for instance, in the "Dance of the Aerialist." The fact was overlooked that each portion of the dance possessed symbolic and even transcendental meaning in terms of the old, traditional religion. Thus, the Christian zealots kept alive the very essence of the polytheistic beliefs which they had sought to destroy.[33]

Gradually, Indigenous dances with themes of Christianity gave birth to the dance-drama of nature. Rather than venerating the earth-goddess in dance, the Indigenous people danced in honor of the Virgin Mary. Similarly, the dances dedicated to the god of spring or the god of corn were performed instead to honor San Isidro, the farmers' patron saint. Such ceremonial Indigenous dances, re-issued with themes from Christian tradition, actually constituted a form of pageant; within the dancing, lengthy dialogues and mock combats were interspersed.[34]

Missionaries augmented the use of masks in ceremonial dance. Because the Indigenous people now needed to portray a white Christian God, Christian saints, and Spanish men, different masks were worn. In the past, the masks used depicted animals or figures unlike the Indigenous people. With the introduction of different prominent characters in the new dance-dramas the use of masks increased. Old masks which could be adapted into the theatrical presentations of Christian themes were the only ones retained.[35]

[32] Covarrubias, p. 34.

[33] Ibid.

[34] Fent Ross, *Made in Mexico,* p.86.

[35] Carlos Navarrete, "Masks," *The Ephemeral and the Eternal of Mexican Folk Art,* Vol. II. (México: Fondo Editorial de la Plastica Mexicana, 1971), p. 742.

The greatest changes effected by the Spanish Conquest in the arts occurred in music. New musical instruments as well as innovative melodies and musical forms were introduced. The guitar had an immediate effect on Indigenous music, as did the flute and other European string instruments like the violin.[36] Today, the guitar is regarded as Mexico's national instrument.

The dances of this period can be described by their thematic content: dance-dramas with Christian themes and dances with polytheistic themes. The dialogue of the characters in dance-dramas depicted important situations, events, and persons.

Dance Dramas with Christian Themes

Spanish priests used Christian themes in dance and plays as a pedagogical device to convert the Indigenous people to Christianity. Traditional dance festivals were well entrenched in Indigenous culture. Thus, by preserving rather than suppressing this tradition, the Church found a more accessible means of rooting itself in the center of community life as well as fostering a positive image of itself.[37]

A variety of plays, comedies, pantomimes, and tableaux about the history of the Indigenous people and the mysteries of their religion provided entertainment for the Spaniards.[38] The oldest, most significant, and most widely-known of these Christian dance-dramas are *Los Moros y Cristianos, Los Santiagos, La Conquista*, and *La Danza de la Pluma*.

Los Moros y Cristianos (The Moors and the Christians)

The first Christian dance-drama to be introduced into Mexico was probably the dance of the "Moors and the Christians." The earliest known record of this dance in Mexico dates from 1524, at which time *Los Moros y Cristianos* was presented to Cortés in Coatzacoalc-

[36] Dickins, p. 6.

[37] Donald Cordry, p. 231

[38] Fergusson, p. 11.

os, Veracruz.[39] This drama symbolized the union of two cultures. The dramatization exemplified the constant struggle of the Indigenous people in deciding between their own ancient traditions and new customs the Spaniards had to offer as a means of survival.

The tradition underlying the story of the Christians and the Moors, loosely associated with a Christian festival, is the epic struggle of good versus evil. The Christians represent the forces of good, whereas the Moors are usually depicted by masked dancers with dark beards symbolizing the anti-Christ or the dark forces of evil.[40]

In this dance-drama, a broad thematic range is presented, with a number of variants: the cycle of Santiago (Saint James); the cycle of Pilate, situated in Jerusalem; the cycle of Granada, based on the re-seizing of Andalusia; and the Carlovingian cycle, featuring the Charlemagne and his force of twelve brave paladins. The plots and characters of these cycles often varied back then from their derived form.[41]

A typical dance-drama today in Mexico involves the following sequences: the ritualistic beginning of the dance requesting sanction for the performance from the church's individual saint; the two opposing groups meeting and engaging in lengthy theological debates; individual struggles between these emissaries, using machetes or swords; and the conversion to Christianity.[42] Most sources have found the battle scene between the Christians and the "heathens" to be the central focus. In historical accounts, Luis Covarrubias, Frances Gillmore, Arthur and Irene Warman, depict variations of the martial

[39] Covarrubias, p. 23.

[40] Lisa Lekis, *Folk Dances of Latin America* (New York: The Scarecrow Press, Inc., 1958), p. 47.

[41] Arthur and Irene Warman, "Dances," *The Ephemeral and the Eternal of Mexican Folk Art*, Vol. II. (México: Fondo Editorial de la Plastica Mexicana, 1971), p. 746.

[42] Arthur and Irene Warman, "Dances," *The Ephemeral and the Eternal of Mexican Folk Art*, Vol. II (México: Fondo Editorial de la Plastica Mexicana, 1971), p. 746.

theme in the dance execution and costuming.

Luis Covarrubias in *Regional Dances of Mexico* presents two versions of the battle scene. One version describes the battle of the Crusades during the time of Charlesmagne. Wooden *machetes* are used in choreographing the combat scene. Lengthy, strange, pointless, complex, and illogical tales are recited throughout the dance-drama. The second version is based on the Moors and Christians dance-drama that is performed on the Pátzcuaro lakeshore. This version exhibits a uniqueness in dance execution. Four dancers, rather than battling with *machetes*, "carry out a vigorous dance step with a rhythm accentuated by the enormous spurs they wore."[43]

Covarrubias' version omits the use of *machetes* or swords in the dramatic conflict between the Moors and the Christians. On the other hand, the Warman's version of the dance retains the use of *palos* or sticks reminiscent of the battle, especially in the states first conquered by the Spaniards: México, Veracruz, Michoacán, and Guana-juato.[44]

In an informative article, "The Dance Dramas of Mexican Villages," Frances Gillmor provides descriptions of the battle scene based on her personal observations of performances in two separate Mexican villages: Ixtapalapa in the Distrito Federal and Tianguistengo in the State of Hidalgo.[45] Restricting her research to the battle scene between Moors and Christians, Gillmor notes that in Ixtapalapa "the dance was usually little more than pacing back and forth with furious flourishes of swords. On occasion the music would strike up, and the movements and swordplay would be swift and rhythmic."[46] In the villages of Tianguistengo "the 'Santiagos' dances without dialogue but with such lightness and swiftness in their leaping sword-

---

[43] Covarrubias, p. 23.

[44] Arthur and Irene Warman, p. 747.

[45] Frances Gillmor, "The Dance Dramas of Mexican Villages," University of Arizona Bulletin, XIV, No. 2 (1943), p. 5.

[46] Ibid., p. 13.

play that their feet hardly seemed to touch the ground."[47]

The costumes are described differently by historians. The Christians are usually more elegantly attired than "heathens." Covarrubias states that the Christians wore ornate and colorful costumes, short trousers, robes or capes, crowns topped with a crucifix, and masks of Spaniards with blonde beards and blue eyes.[48] Gillmor observes that the Christian dancers typically battled without masks; whereas the Moors wore "masks" which were actually false black beards and dark glasses.[49] The Warman's costume description differs from the others in that the use of banners differentiated the two groups of opponents, with the Mexican flag often identifying the Christian side.[50]

Today, the dance of the "Moors and Christians" is more than a single dance. The initial versions were separated from their source and eventually mutated into totally different works. In Mexico alone, many different dances are part of this group: *Danzas Del Marquez, Las Moritas, Los Alchileos, Los Santiagos, Sonajas, Los Matachines, Los Concheros, La Conquista, Los Doce Pares de Francia,* and *Los Tastoanes.*[51] A large number of other dances have also been influenced by the pageantry and dramatic conflict of the Moors and the Christians.

Los Santiagos (Dance of St. James)

A variant of the "Moors and Christians" dance described above in *Los Santiagueros* or *Santiagos*. According to legend prior "to decisive battles between the Spanish and Indians, visions of Santiago ap-

---

[47] Ibid.

[48] Covarrubias, p. 23.

[49] Gillmor, pp. 14-15.

[50] Arthur and Irene Warman, p. 747.

[51] Cordry, p.231.

peared in the sky."[52]

In this dance-drama, Saint James with help from no one converts the "heathens" to Christianity or vanquishes them. Hence the conquest of Mexico is itself brought about by the dance. In effect, in the introduction, the priests admonish the Indigenous people by telling them that if they do not accept the new religion they will risk God's anger.[53]

Dance-drama versions vary from region to region. Some versions have Santiago battling the Moors, others have him fighting the Turks; and still others have him battling virtually all of history's famous "heathens," such as Cain, Pontius Pilate with General Sabarius and his soldiers, and Fierabras together with his group of followers.[54]

The components in the development of this dance-drama are similar to those of the "Moors and the Christians:" a procession of the characters who march onto the stage, a series of dialogues between the emissaries and the Santiago, the combat, and finally the recessional procession. However, the dances themselves are not similar. In the action of the dance a wide variety of spectacular movements is seen: leaps, gallops, walks in all directions, rocking steps, combinations of turns and spins all accompanied by drums and flutes. In the battle scene, Santiago and his enemies express themselves in duel like movements as the two musicians provide suitable rhythm.[55] The dancers, brandishing flashing *machetes* transform the dance into a contest of agility, skill, and endurance.[56]

One of the most distinctive characteristics of this dance-drama is the costume worn by Santiago. A small wooden or cardboard horse is fastened around the dancer's waist giving the appearance

[52] Ibid. p.232.

[53] Covarrubias, p. 25.

[54] Ibid.

[55] Mompradé and Gutiérrez, p. 128.

[56] Lekis, p. 48.

that the dancer is riding a horse. This is "a trick common in Spain" and utilized in a large number of dances to this day.[57]

During the conquest, the horse puzzled the Indigenous people, who believed the animal and the man were a single being. Many considered these beings supernatural. The horse, a symbol of power and prestige, had a great impact on the course of the Spanish Conquest because it afforded the Spanish forces much greater mobility than the Indigenous people afforded. When the first horse was killed, the Indigenous people discovered the nature of the animal. A law in 1528 prohibited the Indigenous people from using horses.[58]

In the remote villages the Santiago dances tend to be more colorful and exciting than those in the centrally located towns. In the Sierra of Puebla, for instance, the cardboard or wooden horse is thought to be so real, that the dancer playing the role of St. James is commissioned to feed and water the horse for an entire year to make certain that the horse will not leave the village.[59] In the Sierra of Nayarit, during the January 1 fiesta, a band of Moors on horseback pursue Santiago as he repeatedly rides his horse, through a selected thoroughfare until he is taken prisoner by the Moors.[60]

The dance-drama version in the village of Costa Grande in Guerrero focuses Cortés dressed as a magnificent *charro* riding an enormous steed composed of reeds, cardboard, and cloth. The opposing *campesinos* are dressed very differently. The peasants resisting Cortés are armed with crude *machetes* and are shielded with woven *sarapes* tied around their chest and over their left shoulder.[61]

A contrasting variation in Oaxaca presents the vanquished Moctezuma and his forces as heroes, wearing elaborate costumes, while the victor Cortés and his dancers are dressed so unappealingly

---

[57] Arthur and Irene Warman, p. 750.

[58] Mompradé and Gutiérrez, p. 128.

[59] Arthur and Irene Warman, p. 750.

[60] Toor, p. 350.

[61] Covarrubias, p. 25.

that they escape virtually unnoticed.[62]

The dance of *Los Santiagueros* is performed today mainly at religious festivals. However, at the secular festival for Independence Day, September 16, *Los Santiagueros*, *Los Moros y Cristianos*, and *La Conquista* are frequently performed by Indigenous groups.[63]

La Conquista (Dance of Conquest)

The Spanish Conquest of Mexico is a milestone in the history of humanity. Many dance themes from that era focus on the powerful effect the conquest had on the Indigenous people. The "Dance of Conquest" incorporates the essence and strength of the Indigenous people in portraying the struggle between Moctezuma and Cortés. In other countries, epic dance-dramas have taken the same theme and centered the conflict around other characters.[64]

Expressing a religious overtone, this historical dance-drama is called many different names: "Dance of the Conquest," the "Aztec Dance," "Chichimec Dance," "Tenochtli Dance," "Plume Dance," "Dance of the Concheros," or "Dance of the *Cuerudos*" (Indigenous people dressed in skins). These are not simply the same dance called by different names, but different dances based on the same theme.[65]

From the Indigenous perspective, the conquest is dramatized as a tragedy, "the destruction of the Indigenous civilization by the Spanish conquistadors." The redeeming conclusion of the tragedy is the arrival of Christianity in Mexico. The characters include the following: Moctezuma (the conquered Aztec king), Hernán Cortés (the Spanish conqueror of Mexico), Malinche (Cortés' interpreter and later mistress), various Indigenous warriors, and Spanish soldiers.[66]

[62] Toor, p. 352.

[63] Arthur and Irene Warman, p. 750.

[64] Ibid. p. 749.

[65] Cordry, p. 226.

[66] Ibid.

Each of the two commanders is accompanied by a leading character: Cortés is accompanied by Malinche, and Moctezuma is accompanied by Cehuapila (characterized as Moctezuma's loyal princess).[67]

Interestingly, the dance drama has an oral text that is spoken aloud and is full of errors in characterizations and time settings. For example, the Spaniards are portrayed as benevolent, religious characters who have no desire for the gold of the "heathens."[68] The text also has a variety of endings. In one version, Moctezuma, Malinche, Chimal, and the kings of Tlaxcala, Cempoala, Xochimilco, and Tonalla are all converted to Christianity and then set free. In another version Moctezuma is kept prisoner; and in yet another, all the "heathens" undergo baptism, and everyone celebrates the conversion.[69]

Depending on the region of the performance and on the dance version depicted, all to none of the characters wear masks; however, most of the time, Malinche wears a mask.[70] Armed with guns, the Spanish characters are typically attired in unattractive suits or in *charro* outfits.[71] In contrast, Moctezuma and his men are lavishly costumed in silk shirt and kerchiefs and other lustrous, rich materials. Their enormous headdresses are made from brightly colored feathers ornamented with beads and mirrors. In Jalisco the dancers of *La Conquista* are dressed in shirts and robes of quality fabrics; their headdresses have feathers, mirrors, and beads.[72]

Performances of this group of conquest dances commonly can be found in villages from Nayarit to Chiapas on days honoring local saints. The most dazzling are presented in Oaxaca and Jalisco.[73]

[67] Mompradé and Gutiérrez, p. 149.

[68] Toor, p. 347.

[69] Mompradé and Gutiérrez. P.149.

[70] Cordry, p. 226.

[71] Mompradé and Gutiérrez, p. 149.

[72] Toor, p. 347.

[73] Ibid.

La Danza de la Pluma (The Feather Dance)

A dance of welcome, "The Feather Dance" reportedly came from various Aztec legends about *Quetzalcóatl,* the plumed serpent-god who had vanished but promised to return eventually. This deity's symbolic bird, the *quetzal*, furnished the elaborate plumage for both royalty and priests. In spite of his beard and moustache, Cortés, who had light hair and fair skin, was believed to resemble the *Quetzalcóatl.*[74]

Features in the costume suggest the figure of a spectacular, crested bird, *Quetzalcocochtli*, "the bird that sings at dawn." The crested bird portrays an image of the deity *Macuilxochitl* "whose feast, *Xochilhuitl*, festival of the flowers," continues to be celebrated in Oaxaca. According to Luis Covarrubias, Mexico's leading costume and dance historian, this costume feature and other details in *La Danza de la Pluma* confirm that this dance probably was derived from a ritual honoring *Macuilochitl*, the god of song, music, dance, and court nobility.[75]

"The Feather Dance" mimics the theme of the "Christians and the Moors" in depicting Moctezuma as the good in conflict with Cortés as the evil.[76] The characters of *La Danza de la Pluma* typically include the historical figures of Moctezuma, Cortés, Malinche, Cehuapila, Icotil, and Pedro de Alvarado (a Lieutenant of Cortés who ordered the massacre known as the *noche triste*).[77] These characters depict the historical events which occurred during the Spanish Conquest of Tenochtitlán, the Aztec capital. The opening scene shows Moctezuma and Cehuapila as resisting the Spaniards; this is followed

---

[74] Rosa Guerrero, "Value Clarification of the Chicano Culture Through Music and Dance," Lecture at a symposium sponsored by the Texas Committee for the Humanities and Mexican American Studies Program at the University of Houston Central Campus, 1979.

[75] Covarrubias, p. 16.

[76] Arthur and Irene Warman, p. 749.

[77] Covarrubias, p. 16.

by a grave battle which results in the conquered Aztec king being imprisoned. In the dance intervals, pantomime and dialogue are presented.[78]

Today, the most popular versions of this dance-drama are found in the states of Jalisco and Oaxaca. Similarities and variations of this dance exist in the villages of Oaxaca due to the importance given to the main characters in the text, costuming, and dance interpretation in each area.

Augustín Hernández describes a vivid version of this dance-drama that appears in *historia general del arte mexicano.* In his narrative, Hernández, a dance-master of San Martin Tilcajete in Oaxaca, gives a historical and personal orientation to the various actions of the dance:

> The dance-drama begins with a drum roll and the sounds of the rattles made by the dancers. The captain or dance master begins the presentation by dedicating the dance-drama to the ruler Moctezuma, who was tortured and imprisoned by Cortés and his troops with the help of nobles of Tlaxcala on the thirteenth of August, 1521. He invites the kings and nobles in the drama to dance with eagerness to the rhythm of the melodic sounds of the musical accompaniment in honor of all those present.
>
> Cortés and Malinche appear sitting on side of the stage area with Moctezuma and Cehuapila sitting on the opposite side. The dance-drama consists of the following acts which appear in the history of the conquest: the *registro*, signifying the entrance of the Aztecs to Tenochtitlán; the *himno*, a self-expressive dance of joy for being present at the designated place requested by their ruler; the *chotis*, a schottische dance they were accustomed to performing before their ruler; a dance performed by the Captains followed by the monks who perform a war-like dance (using leaps, jumps, kneels while covering spaces) in preparation for the battle; the *espacio*, the announcement that Cortés had landed in Veracruz; the *marcha*, the first entrance of Cortés in Tenochtitlán (signifying *la noche triste* in Mexican history); the dance *mis cantares*, which symbolize the first envoy sent by

[78] Arthur and Irene Warman, p. 749.

Moctezuma to interview Cortés and vice-versa; the *marcha*, representing the appearance of Cortés trying to oppress Moctezuma; the performance of *cuadrillas* (quadrilles): *Tres al fondo* (three in the rear); the *hincadas* (the kneels) accompanied by hand rattles, which they enjoyed dancing for Moctezuma; the *marinero* dance, depicting the first battle of Cortés upon entering Moctezuma's palace; the *registro*, the demolished palace after the struggle between Cortés and Moctezuma; and Moctezuma being taken prisoner.[79] (translated and edited for clarity by Sanjuanita Martínez-Hunter)

In two different villages of Oaxaca importance is given to the main characters in the text and dance interpretation. For instance, in one version Malinche is portrayed by a young girl, who wears an ordinary dress, but a fancy headpiece. Malinche performs a solo dance in which she is linked to Moctezuma rather than Cortés. The other dancers execute light, graceful movement to the musical accompaniment of the rattles they carry. Their movements represent an interpretation of both the rhythm and the dance-steps of the *jota* of Spain (a folk dance) and the *chotis* (or the schottische which is a European ballroom dance).[80]

A distinct interpretation is presented in another village in Oaxaca. In this version one of the most beautiful dances in the work is performed by Moctezuma. First, each of the warriors lays down his spear. Moctezuma then dances down the length of the line and back with a swiftness, grace, and agility. On his way back, Moctezuma picks up and hands a spear to every owner. This movement symbolizes the king's arming of his men against the invading Spaniards.[81]

As this dance-drama progresses, the dominating character of Malinche, also known as Malintzin or Marina, intervenes. The characters of Malinche on the side of Cortés, and Cehuapila on the side of Moctezuma, are represented by two young girls. Cehuapila is garbed

---

[79] Mompradé and Gutiérrez, p. 152.

[80] Toor, p. 347.

[81] Fergusson, p. 98.

in feathers and skins. At a given point in the dance, both of these young girls come face-to-face, using gliding/crossing movements to depict a struggle. In this context Malinche hoists the Mexican flag of today.[82] It is interesting to note that in these two separate episodes a man does not interpret the female role. In the majority of dances, a man disguises himself as a woman to portray the role of the Malinche.

Focusing on the costume and dance details of this drama, Luis Covarrubias perceived the vestiges of an ancient ritual: for instance in the dance, the solemn bowing in the introduction to each of the four cardinal directions and the cordate scepter grasped in the dancer's left hand; and in the costuming, the huge headdress trimmed with mirrors and adorned with plumes, the brilliantly hued cape, the pantaloons with silk bands and gold fringe, and the apron bedecked with medals and coins of silver. From such evidence, Covarrubias concludes that the dance's "modern significance is only a disguise for an ancient ceremonial rite." [83]

These historical and martial dance-dramas intertwined with Christianity afford the Mexican people an opportunity to "develop a positive image" of their Indigenous heritage.[84] Furthermore, these dances provide an expression of the antipathy that was and continues to be expressed toward the Spanish conquerors and rulers. In comparing the masks and costume of the Indigenous people to the Spaniards the empathy toward the Indigenous plight is obvious. Beautiful costumes help characterize the Indigenous people as dignified; while ill-fitting, tasteless costumes characterize the Spanish conquerors as brutes.[85]

[82] Mompradé and Gutiérrez, p. 152.

[83] Covarrubias, p.16.

[84] Cordry, p. 228.

[85] Ibid.

Dances with Polytheistic Themes

Despite the fact that ceremonial dancing was not a common practice in the Catholic Church, Spanish missionaries allowed the Indigenous people to perform the *tocotín* in their churches. This Indigenous song-dance with poetic overtones was so admired for its beauty that the priests deemed it an appropriate form of worship even inside the church.[86] With little modification, the Spanish priests incorporated Indigenous dances together with costuming and musical accompaniment into their Christian worship. Many times in their songs the only changes were names of Indigenous gods replaced by the names of Catholic saints.[87]

The Christianization of the Indigenous people was facilitated by this process. Priests exploited the parallels that could be drawn between Catholicism and the Aztec religion. By studying these similarities, the polytheistic themes which predominate many ritualistic dances become evident. The reason why it was to the priests' advantage to blend the ceremonies into a new form of worship in the Christianizing process will be evident also.

The following are listed parallels between the ancient Aztec religion and the new Catholic religion imposed upon the Indigenous people:

1. The Aztecs worshipped several minor gods. The Catholics worshipped only one God, but venerated many saints.[88]
2. In *La Danza de la Pluma*, *Quetzalcóatl* is welcomed back to Mexico. Legend promised his return to his people. The *quetzal*, a luxuriously plumed bird symbolized this god.[89]Catholic teachings promises the return of Jesus to his people. Also the Holy Ghost, a person of the Trinity, is symbolized by the

---

[86] Portia Mansfield, "The Conchero Dancers of Mexico" (Ed.D. dissertation, New York University, 1953), p. 122.

[87] Fent Ross, *Made in Mexico,* p. 86.

[88] Mansfield, p. 122.

[89] Guerrero, lecture at a symposium.

dove. Many times, in Catholic paintings and sculptures, angels are depicted as winged creatures.

3. Both Aztecs and Catholics schedule religious festivals in accordance with their respective calendars.[90] For the Indigenous people, dates had much more symbolic meaning. For Catholics "saints' days" were as meaningful as birthdays.

4. A legend which relates the darkening of the sky and the appearance of a rose colored cross in the sky is linked to the defeat of the Otomís by the Spaniards and their allies.[91] It was this phenomenon which helped convert the Chichimecas. The day becoming dark can be explained by the fact that a solar eclipse occurred on July 25, 1532.[92] A similar darkening of the sky purportedly occurred on Good Friday, when Jesus died on the cross.

5. Goddesses were worshiped by the Aztecs.[93] For Catholics, the Virgen Mary held a position of high esteem. On December 12, 1531, the Virgen appeared to Juan Diego at the site where the Basílica of the Virgin of Guadalupe stands today. The patron saint of Mexico, a brown Indigenous Virgen, the blend of two cultures, is celebrated yearly by various Indigenous dances including the Concheros which began when Querétaro was overthrown.

6. The thorns and wounds symbolically associated with the Aztec god of war played an important part in the crucifixion of Christ.[94]

7. The cross is a symbol that transfers from one religion to the other. The Aztecs paid homage to the four cardinal points,

[90] Mansfield, p. 101.

[91] Covarrubias, p. 14.

[92] Martha Stone. *At the Sign of Midnight* (Arizona: The University of Arizona Press, 1975), p.97.

[93] Mansfield, p. 102.

[94] Ibid., p. 103.

the four directions, or the four winds in the sign of the cross. Catholics carry crucifixes and begin prayers with the Sign of the Cross.

8. The use of incense, for purification, flower offerings to deities, decoration of altars, and good luck charms or gold medals is common in both religions.[95]

9. Surprisingly enough, the one ritual to which the Spanish priests objected the most, human sacrifice, drew a strong parallel to the Catholic sacrament of the Holy Eucharist. The Eucharist is symbolic of Christ's body and blood, His sacrifice to redeem man. In effect, this was the ultimate human sacrifice.[96]

10. Both faiths made use of pilgrimages, music, dance, dramas, processions, banners, utensils of gold and silver, beautiful robes made of rich materials embroidered in gold, and much finery.[97]

Because of the existing parallels, it was advantageous to the Spanish priests to utilize ritual to draw the Indigenous people to Christianity. The less change that could occur, the less threatening the conversion would seem.

The dances of the Concheros illustrate particularly well the intertwining of the Indigenous customs with Christian beliefs. These elements enhance the symbolism of the movements and the thematic context of the dances. In modern Mexico, modified polytheistic aspects remain a part of the dances of the Concheros. In the next section these dances are examined more closely.

[95] Ibid. p. 106.

[96] Ibid., p. 104.

[97] Ibid., p. 106.

La Danza de los Concheros (The Concheros Dance)

A number of dances are clearly reminiscent of the Concheros, an Indigenous group of people who inhabited Central Mexico in ancient times.[98] Described in their songs as "soldiers of the Conquest of the Holy Religion," the name of these legendary figures, "concheros," is derived from the musical instrument associated with them, a mandolin or guitar fabricated from the shell-like protective armor, or *concha*, of the armadillo, an animal regarded as a symbol of the earth.[99]

Undoubtedly historically rooted, the dances of the Concheros began about 1522, amidst the conquest of Querétaro. During this event, the Spaniards and the Otomí overcame the Chichimecas, (synonymous with Concheros), and made Christians of them. It is believed that those dances were created to disguise the polytheistic customs and beliefs of the Chichimecas in their new worship. Even today, polytheistic motifs predominate their rituals and dances.[100]

Legends and historical accounts state that the Indigenous people first danced in veneration of Christianity at the time of the battle in Tlaxcala. Known also as Sangremal, (blood bath), this battle was named after a hill in Querétaro which was the site of this particularly bloody struggle. The Concheros' origins are traditionally attributed to the Spanish victory over certain nomadic tribes, at this hill of Sangremal and to the transfer of Our Lady of Guadalupe's image to the sanctuary that is now named for her.[101]

In her book *At the Sign of Midnight*, Martha Stone provides a version of the Concheros' beginnings. This particular version was told to her by modern descendants of the conquered inhabitants who still live in Querétaro. Refugio Piñedo narrates the origin of the Concheros:

[98] Covarrubias, p. 14.

[99] Dickins, p. 7.

[100] Ibid.

[101] Arthur and Irene Warman, p. 743.

The Spaniards were camping just outside Tlaxcala when Cortés announced that on a certain day he would make his entrance into the city he had conquered. The Tlaxcalans began to prepare for a big fiesta in his honor on that day. It was at that time that a commission of *danzantes* from Tlaxcala went to Cortés to ask permission to dance at this big fiesta. Cortés gave them permission to do so, if they would dance in honor of their Christian idols. That day was the first time they danced as Christians.[102] [edited for clarity by Sanjuanita Martínez-Hunter]

After this victory, on September 23, 1519, Xicotencatl, Tlaxcala's ruler, one of the four principal rulers of the Republic, formally received Cortés at his palace. Historical sources relate that the Spaniards stayed in Tlaxcala for six weeks. According to Historian Helen Banks, who wrote *The History of Mexico* on the day of their departure to Cholula,

> ...they had scarcely left the city of Tlaxcala when a thin, transparent cloud settled down over the cross the Christians had erected in the temple courtyard and wrapped the cross in soft folds, which shone all through the night with a clear light, thus proving to the Indians the truth and power of the religion of the white conquerors.[103]

In Martha Stone's interview, Refugio Piñedo also relates a legend which tells of the Concheros being present in Tlaxcala during the sight:

> The Sangremal was the famous battle where Spaniards conquered Querétaro. Querétaro was conquered for the Spaniards by a great Chichimeca general. At the time of his conversion to the Catholic religion and baptism, they changed his name from Conin to Fernando de Tapia.

[102] Stone, p. 197.

[103] Helen Ward Banks, *The History of Mexico* (New York: Frederick A. Stokes Company, 1926), p. 118.

This great Chichimeca general gave orders for the Spaniards and the Chichimecas to fight, but to fight without their
arms. The Spaniards could not use their guns or their horses
while the Chichimecas could not use their bows and arrows or
their slings. As they fought they kicked, scratched, birth with
their teeth, pulled hair, and they gouged each other's eyes out
with their thumbs. The blood flowed in streams.

While they were fighting the day became dark, almost like
night, and there appeared in the sky a rose-colored cross. Eve-
rybody fell on their knees to worship this cross thus ending the
famous Battle of Sangremal.

During the fighting, the great General Conin was sitting on
his horse, on the mountainside, watching the battle. On the
ground beside him stood a Chichimeca with his bow and arrow.
In front of him stood a Conchero playing his concha. This proves
that Concheros were present during the battle.[104] [edited for
clarity by Sanjuanita Martínez-Hunter]

This legendary tale has a historical foundation. After Neza-
hualpilli the chief of Texcoco died in 1516, Moctezuma promoted
Cacama. Cacama ruled Texcoco from the time of the invasion of the
Spaniards to the time of his death during the great smallpox epidemic. He was followed by Coanacoch (Serpent Ear Plug). Coanacoch
ruled in Texcoco until the end in 1520, when Cortés conquered this
city. Under the rule of Cortés, Ixtlixochitl, a brother of the vanquished ruler became the new chief of Texcoco. Not long after becoming chief he was converted to Christianity and baptized as Don
Fernando.[105]

The dances of the Concheros, together with the devotion to the
cross or to the four winds, appear to have come from one of the early
miracles which helped convert the Indigenous peoples. The
Concheros legend growing out of the Battle of Sangremal on July 25,
1531, is also discussed by Frances Toor, the Mexican folklorist, and
by the Mexican dance historians, Arthur and Irene Warman. Accord-

[104] Stone, pp. 197-198.

[105] Peterson, p. 103.

ing to Toor and the Warmans it is evident that in the midst of the most furious fighting between Chichimecas and Christians a cross and an image of the Apostle Santiago (Saint James) appeared in the heavens.[106] Recognizing that a more powerful force was indeed counterpoised against them, the Chichimecas asked the victorious Spanish to erect a crucifix as a landmark on the field of battle. They named this site "Sangremal" as a reminder of all the bloodshed. In honor of the power of this cross, the Indigenous people celebrated by dancing around it for a week. [107]

A typical contemporary Conchero dance troupe has a paramilitary organization governed by strict rules and punitive consequences for infractions. Whereas, the roles of women were portrayed by men in earlier dances, in the Concheros troupe females were admitted into the ranks to portray the historical figure of Malinche.[108] In the mystery plays used to Christianize the Indigenous people, the Spanish priests cast females in female roles. Seeing women act in these mystery plays precipitated the casting of females to portray Malinche.[109]

The ritual of the dance of the Concheros is traditionally separated into three major divisions: the *velacíon* (vigil before the dance), the sanctioning of the performance, and the dance itself. Throughout the vigil, *alabanzas* (songs of praise) are sung to the souls of dead dancers. Once at the church, the dancers obtain permission from the pastor to dedicate their dance to the patron saint of that church. The dancers then greet the house of worship and request the sanction of the patron saint to perform in the sanctuary. Next the dancers appease the gods by reverently offering their performance to the four cardinal points.[110]

[106] Arthur and Irene Warman, p. 743.

[107] Toor, p. 329.

[108] Momprodé and Gutiérrez, pp. 162-163.

[109] Fent Ross, *Made in Mexico*, p. 87.

[110] Momprodé and Gutiérrez, pp. 162-163.

The dance itself begins with a ritual shout, "He is God!" As the dance leader gives the shout he simultaneously forms a sign of the cross with both feet. The dancers form a circle with the dancers of higher rank in the center.[111] The dance pattern begins with the "cross," "a measure in which the dancers draw this symbol with their feet."[112] To execute the steps of this dance, the dancers hop,

> on one foot while making a cross in the air with the other; crossing the feet with a rocking from side to side; jumping into the air and landing on their toes like a rooster; make genuflections, and certain percussive steps.[113]

Their agile, charming performance ends with forceful stomping on the ground.[114]

Through the years, the costumes for these dances have been transformed to often imitate Aztec noblemen's clothes. Mompradé and Gutiérrez list the following components in the traditional Conchero costume:

> *penachos*--- the leather headdresses with the trimming of the beads of tinfoil, spangles, and mirrors, and surmounted by long feathers of brilliant colors; the *pectoral*—breastcloth; the *maxtle*—a spangled, knee-length skirt or tunic; *rodilleros*—knee-guards; *brazaletes*—bracelets; plus stockings and sandals.[115]

All dancers wear similar costumes, except the one portraying the devil. The devil wears a crimson suit and a mask.[116] Both the

---

[111] Toor, p. 328.

[112] Arthur and Irene Warman, p. 744.

[113] Dickins, p. 8.

[114] Toor, p. 328.

[115] Mompradé and Gutiérrez, p. 163.

[116] Covarrubias, p. 14.

male and the female dancers wear long-haired wigs in imitation of the ancient Chichimecas.[117] The musical accompaniment is provided by the guitars made of armadillo shells, mandolins, a *huehuetl* and a *teponaztli*. Rhythm is provided by *ayoyotes* or *huesos* (strings of seeds tied to the dancers' feet) and rattles.[118]

In this and other dance-dramas, it is evident how the religious rituals of ancient times merged with the cultural influence introduced by the Spaniards to mold Mexico's dance heritage. The Spanish missionaries used those elements of the Indigenous religion that served their purpose to Christianize the people. Little did the priests suspect that in allowing the *tocotín* to be performed inside their first missions they allowed the integration of Catholic ceremonies by Indigenous religious rituals. The Indigenous people were more sophisticated than the Spanish priests suspected.

[117] Toor, p. 327.

[118] Arthur and Irene Warman, p. 744.

CHAPTER 3: DANCE IN MEXICO (1525-1810) - THE SPANISH COLONIZATION

The colonial period was characterized by expansion and growth. The art, music, dance, literature and philosophy of New Spain sometimes rivaled that of Spain itself.[1] The colonial period began with the conquest of the Aztecs by the Spanish forces under Hernán Cortés. His second expedition began in 1519, and after three years of conflict, the conquest was completed. From 1521 until independence was achieved in 1821, three centuries later, Mexico was officially a member of the Spanish Empire.[2]

Following the conquest, the Spanish administration's major objectives were to maintain absolute power over the country and to extort its riches, whereas the Catholic Church's motive was to Christianize the Indigenous population. These objectives were embodied in a policy or system called *encomiendos*, originally initiated by Cortés as a means of paying those who had served with him during the conquest of Mexico. This system accorded every Spaniard an allotment of Indigenous people whom he must feed and clothe as well as Christianize; in exchange, the Indigenous people were obligated to work for their masters.[3] The Spanish masters, however, greatly abused the Indigenous people. In their lust to acquire great wealth, they forced the Indigenous people into slavery and threated them so cruelly that hundreds perished as they labored in the fields and mines. When it became obvious that the Indigenous people could not bear up under the harsh conditions and tyrannical practices imposed

---

[1] Smith, p. 169.

[2] *Encyclopedia Britannica,* XV (1972), S.v. "Mexico."

[3] Meyer and Sherman, p. 131.

on them, the conquerors imported Africans as laborers.[4] It was not until 1829 that slavery was finally abolished.[5]

Spain completely controlled the politics, economics, culture, and religion of the Indigenous people. Foreign laws and customs were forced upon them. For their protection an *audiencia* (court with judicial inquiry) was established,[6] but the *audiencias* did not always remain true to the purpose for which they were established. The rule of viceroys, which superseded the *audiencias*, began with Antonio de Mendoza in 1535 and ended in 1821 with Juan O'Donoju. Of the sixty-two viceroys who ruled Mexico during this period of time, only three were of Mexican birth. As might be expected, some viceroys were more humane than others in their treatment of the Mexicans and the Indigenous people.[7]

The Spanish Inquisition, with its fierce censorship powers, arrived in Mexico in the year 1571 under the auspices of Archbishop Pedro Moya de Contreras, who later became viceroy in 1584. The Court of the Inquisition imposed cruel sentences on persons judged immoral, heretic, or treacherous. At times prisoners were immolated at the stake. The Inquisitional tribunal was much hated in both the New World and in Spain.[8] Its reign of terror was finally officially abolished in 1820.[9]

Fray Bartolomé de las Casas spoke against the atrocities committed by the Spanish in the name of morality. Under his direction in 1572, a remarkable edict was written, titled *New Laws of the Indies for the Good Treatment and Preservation of the Indians*. "This was written three hundred years before Abraham Lincoln's Emancipa-

[4] Banks, p. 322.

[5] *Encyclopedia Britannica,* XV (1981), S.v. "Mexico," p. 95.

[6] *Collier's Encyclopedia,* XVI (1981), S.v. "Mexico," p. 95.

[7] Meyer and Sherman, p. 155.

[8] Zabre, p. 166.

[9] Meyer and Sherman, p. 199.

tion Proclamation."[10] "The Indian," it announced, "is henceforth free... To enslave them or to mistreat them in anyway is a misdemeanor punishable by law."[11] This edict also included objectionable laws, but nothing came of the edict; it was never enforced.[12]

Unfortunately, an overwhelming body of evidence shows that the Spanish Conquest of Mexico was one of the most brutal occurrences in the New World. This evidence includes: the official records contained in the *Archivos de los Indios* in Spain and the *Archivos de Nueva España* in Mexico; the historical narratives of New Spain compiled by Bernardino de Sahagún and various other priests during the sixteenth century; Cortés' five letters dispatched to Emperor Charles V; the literary contributions of Bernal Díaz del Castillo, Alonso de Molina, Toribio de Benavente (alias Motolínia), Francisco López de Gómara, Diego de Durán, Geronimo de Mendieta, Diego de Landa; and historical narratives written in the seventeenth century by the friars Juan de Torquemada and Francisco Javier de Clavigero.[13]

Criticism and discontent grew, at first cautiously, but eventually in daring publications "three centuries of slavery"[14] and barbarity were denounced. Even popular poetry and songs satirized their conditions. A number of events and practices—especially the importation of slaves and the exploitation of both the Indigenous people and the Africans, the implementation of the caste system, and the limitation of employment to whites—fanned the flames of discontent. Eventually, the time came when the situation became unbearable. On September 15, 1810, the Revolution burst into reality under the

[10] John Patrick McHenry, *A Short History of Mexico* (New York: Doubleday., 1970), p. 44.

[11] Ibid.

[12] Ibid.

[13] Smith, p. 171.

[14] Meyer and Sherman, p. 276.

leadership of Miguel Hidalgo y Costilla, a Catholic priest.[15] Hidalgo, taking the banner of the Virgin de Guadalupe as the emblem of his political crusade, made his famous speech known as the *grito de Dolores,* which in essence proclaimed "Long live Our Lady of Guadalupe! Death to bad government! Death to the gachupines!"[16] (A *gachupine* was a derogatory name given to the Spanish-born people in Mexico).[17]

A major setback occurred during the first attempt to spark the revolutionary spirit for Hidalgo was captured on July 30, 1811. His execution and decapitation extinguished the initial revolutionary flame. The leadership though passed to another friar, this time a *mestizo* (Indigenous-Spanish mixture with Indigenous blood dominating)[18] named José María Morelos y Pavón.[19] "Hidalgo gave the revolutionary movement inspiration. Morelos had given it purpose!"[20]

Major historical events in the history of the conquest are outlined in Table Three. The relationship of these events and the development of dance in Mexico during this period of time is then discussed.

[15] Smith, p. 15.

[16] Meyer and Sherman, p. 288.

[17] Ibid., p. 207.

[18] Ibid., p. 204.

[19] Bradley Smith, *Mexico: A History in* Art (New York: Doubleday and Company, Inc., 1968), p. 210.

[20] Ibid., p. 212.

Table Three
Historical Chronology

1519-1538	There was a decline of many Indigenous artistic customs in this period, but the *mestizo* folk music developed with the blending of the Spanish and Indigenous culture.[21]
1519-1650	Between these years, African slaves were brought into Mexico to share labor with the Indigenous people. African music and dances influenced the country at that time.[22]
1521-1821	During this period, laws were created to protect the Spanish industries. Colonial government was almost entirely in the hands of the Spaniards. The Indigenous population, *mestizos*, and *criollos* had very limited political rights. Toward the end of the eighteenth century, there was a significant movement among intellectuals in the Americas to arouse a spirit of nationalism in the colonies. All these events led to the succession of revolutions in the New World.[23]
1526	European dance music made its appearance in Mexico when Juan Ortiz, a companion of Cortés, petitioned the authorities to grant him permission to open a dancing school "for the embellishment of the city."[24] He taught the chaconne and the sarabande, two pre-classic dance forms.

[21] Stevenson, p. 58.

[22] Banks, p. 322.

[23] Fent Ross, *Made in Mexico*, p. 295.

[24] Slonimsky, p. 220.

| 1527 | (December) Cortés returned to the court of Charles V with a group of Indigenous entertainers who performed for the court. As a result, the pavane, a pre-classic dance form is believed by some to have started.[25] |

1527 — (December) Cortés returned to the court of Charles V with a group of Indigenous entertainers who performed for the court. As a result, the pavane, a pre-classic dance form is believed by some to have started.[25]

Pedro de Gante, a Flemish Franciscan friar, established the first school of music in Texcoco.[26]

1528 — Fray Juan de Zumárraga was appointed the first bishop of Mexico. He encouraged the founding of schools where reading, writing, and music were taught to the Indigenous people.[27]

1531 — (December 12) Juan Diego had a vision of the Virgin of Guadalupe on the hill of Tepeyac.[28]

1532 — The Spanish *autos* (religious plays with music) were introduced in Mexico by the Spanish friars. These medieval mysteries did not succeed in winning converts.[29]

1535 — Antonio Mendoza, the first viceroy of New Spain, arrived in Mexico. He ruled for fifteen years.

[25] *The New Grove Dictionary of Music and Musicians,* XII (1980), S.v. "Mexico."

[26] Stevenson, p. 53.

[27] Ibid., p. 58.

[28] Smith, p. 169.

[29] Gilbert Chase, *The Music of Spain* (New York: W.W. Norton and Company, 1943) pp. 271-272.

1536	(January 7) The College of Santa Cruz de Tlatelolco for Indians started with sixty students who were taught reading, writing, Latin grammar, rhetoric, philosophy, and music.[30]
1540	An Indigenous singer from the city of Tlaxcala composed a mass.[31]
1542	Charles I of Spain forbade Indigenous slavery and restricted colonists' control over the Indigenous people.[32]
1547	(December 2) Cortés died on his last trip to Spain at the age of sixty-three. [33]
1550	The Dominican friar Bartolomé de las Casas abolished Indigenous slavery.[34]
1553	(January 25) Luis Velasco I, the second viceroy in Mexico, established the University of Mexico. [35]
1555	Charles V prohibited any type of dancing before the noon Sunday mass. Banners, masks, songs of ancient rites were forbidden by the Mexican

[30] Stevenson, p. xii.

[31] *The New Grove Dictionary of Music and Musicians*, XII (1980) S.v. "Mexico."

[32] Smith, p. 169.

[33] McHenry, p. 40.

[34] Stevenson, p. 64.

[35] Ibid., p. xii.

Church Council. [36]

1556	Twelve liturgical books containing music were published in Mexico between 1560 and 1589.[37]
1571	The Spanish Inquisition was established under Mexico under Bishop Moya de Contreras.[38]
1579	The performances of the sarabande was prohibited.[39]
1585	The Mexican Church Council forbade the Indigenous people from wearing *coronas* or headdresses made from white, turkey feathers because they manifested idolatry.[40]
1623	The Sacred Office of the Inquisition in the province of Zapotitlán informed superiors of the continued practice of "iniquitous and pagan" dances among the Yaqui people. This office recommended a five hundred ducats fine and deportation of the Indigenous people from their pueblos.[41]
1711	Manuel Zumaya produced at the Viceroy's palace the first opera in Mexico, "Partenope," written by a native. It was performed in Italian because of the

[36] Ibid., p. 64.

[37] Ibid., p. 68.

[38] Zabre, p. 166.

[39] Stevenson, p. 29.

[40] Stone, p. 193.

[41] Slonimsky, p. 213.

Italian domination of Mexican music.[42]

1753	The Coliseo theater was erected in New Spain.[43]
1767	The Jesuits were expelled from New Spain.[44]
1779	Dancing was prohibited for both sexes in salons. Musicians who played for mixed dancing were sent to prison for six months.[45]
1789	The first *pan de jarabe* (song-dance) was introduced and later denounced by the Inquisition.[46]
1790	(July 9) The *jarabe* was presented for the first time in Mexico City at the Coliseo theater.[47]
1791-1794	Theatrical dance in Mexico had its beginning.[48]
1802	The Inquisition of Mexico forbade the performance of the *jarabe gatuno* because of the indecent words sung with the dance.[49]
1805	The *zarzuela,* a Spanish operetta, was introduced in

[42] Ibid., p. 220.

[43] Stevenson, p. 184.

[44] Smith, p. 169.

[45] Slonimsky, p. 220.

[46] Stevenson, p. 184.

[47] Ruíz, p. 47.

[48] Ibid., p. 56.

[49] Meyer and Sherman, pp. 230-231.

Mexico. On October 1, the first issue of *Diario de México*, a daily newspaper, was published.[50]

1810   (September 15 and 16) The *grito de Dolores*, or the cry for independence, was proclaimed by the parish priest, Miguel Hidalgo y Costilla at the village of Dolores.

Pictured above are dancers of the UT Ballet Folklorico performing *sones* from the state of Yucatán, Mexico on campus during the late 1970s. Photo courtesy of the Sanjuanita Martínez-Hunter Collection.

[50] Stevenson, p. 74.

DEVELOPMENT OF DANCE

It has been said that "Mexican arts are not the product of the Spanish influence on an Indian foundation so much as of Indian influence on a Spanish foundation."[51] During the colonial era, Mexican folklore represented the product of two fundamental strains: Old World traditions in a New World and New World traditions in an Old World.[52]

As language problems between the Spaniards and the Indigenous people diminished, so did the use of drama as a means of conveying Christian doctrine.[53] Mexican themes began to replace the Spanish historical and Christian dance-dramas. The *Danza de los Tocotínes*, the *Danza de los Negritos*, and the *Danza de los Torteros* reflected the religious, political, and economic situation that existed during the era. The theme of *La Danza de los Tocotínes* emanated from the policy of *encomenderos*,[54] deriving its name from the *tocotín*. This musical form was linked to Biblical stories in the Náhuatl (Aztec) language.[55] Labor on a sugar plantation was the theme of *La Danza de los Negritos* (The Dance of the Black Men).[56] *La Danza de los Torteros* (The Dance of the Miners) commemorated forced labor of the Indigenous people in the Spaniard's silver and gold mining operations.[57]

[51] Rodney Gallop, "The Music of Indian Mexico," *Musical Quarterly*, XXV (1939), p. 210.

[52] Funk and Wagnall, *Standard Dictionary of Folklore-Mythology Legend*, 1972 ed., S.v. "Mexican and Central American Indian Folklore," by George M. Foster.

[53] Fent Ross, "Regional Dances of Mexico," p. 36.

[54] Lekis, p. 48.

[55] Arthur and Irene Warman, p. 752.

[56] Ibid., p. 747.

[57] Lekis, p. 49.

The rural areas continued to incorporate masks in their dances. The *tigre danzas* (the tiger dances), known as *La Danza de los Tecuanes* (The Dance of the Wild Beast) and *La Danza de los Tlacoleros*, a dance dedicated to a man who prepares the land for cultivation in the slash-and-burn method, were the most popular masked dances of the era.[58] The *danza*, a rural dance form of the times, gave birth to the *mestizo* regional dance.[59]

Dance and music, as art forms, became much more popular than the former dramatic enactments in Mexico. It was not until the latter part of the seventeenth century, however, that a completely secular theatrical art form, totally separate from ecclesiastical purposes, developed. It was at this point that the colonies began to become aware of the works of dramatists such as Calderón de la Barca and Lope de Vega.[60]

Initially the court circles and aristocratic surroundings of the viceroys were the target audience of such works. From the eighteenth century, however, they began to appear in the opera houses and theaters of more sizable communities such as Mexico City's Teatro Coliseo, which existed from its opening in 1670 until its destruction by fire in 1722.[61]

In local repertoire, several dramatic art forms persisted into the start of the nineteenth century, at least until the year 1805. These included: Carnival themes, prevailing in the dramatic arts;[62] the *zarzuela*, a buffa or farcical type of dramatic work common to local rep-

[58] Arthur and Irene Warman, p. 750.

[59] *The New Grove Dictionary of Music and Musicians,* XII (1980), S.v. "Mexico."

[60] Gérard Béhague, *Music in Latin America: an Introduction* (New Jersey: Prentice-Hall., 1979), p. 60.

[61] Ibid.

[62] *The New Grove Dictionary of Music and Musicians,* XII (1980), S.v. "Mexico."

ertoire;[63] the *tonadilla*, a short skit performed by two characters which occurs between two acts of a play or entr'acte;[64] the *sainete*, a type of farce designed to end an evening at the theater;[65] and the *entremése*, a type of burlesque interlude performed as an entr'acte.[66] Thus, a high degree of diversity distinguished the entertainment of an evening. As interludes in the *zarzuelas*, popular Mexican dances and songs were utilized.[67] These interludes, mentioned in the *Diario de México* in 1806 as "bailes del país," consisted of short dances utilized to lengthen the evening's performance.[68]

When the political disorders began to form at the beginning of the nineteenth century, the diversity of entertainment in New Spain began to disappear. The Mexican people had other preoccupations than attending the theater, organizing masquerades or composing new styles of music to accompany the dance. The dance of this era took into consideration the historical, the geographical, and the ethnological circumstances that worked directly on the artistic phenomenon.[69]

During the Spanish colonization of Mexico, people from many ethnic groups arrived in the New World and contributed to the secular music and dance of Mexico. West African slaves and the broad communication with Africans who lived in the Caribbean particularly influenced the character of regional Mexican music and dance.[70] Furthermore, the culture of immigrants from Britain, France, Germany,

[63] Béhague, p. 60.

[64] Stevenson, p. 174.

[65] Ibid.

[66] Ibid.

[67] Béhague, p. 61.

[68] Ibid.

[69] Weinstock (ed.), *Mexican Music,* p. 10.

[70] *The Encyclopedia Americana,* XVIII (1983), S.v. "Mexico."

Italy, and other European nations, as well as from Asia, influenced the Mexican performing arts.[71] But, Spain's music and dance always made the greatest impact on Mexican art forms. Although a great amount of the music and dance reflected the cultural heritage that made the New World so immensely versatile most Indigenous people deliberately maintained their cultural identity.[72]

The Dance of the Cosmic Race

By way of Spain, there came to Mexico a variety of musical traditions: Italian, German, French, and Moorish-Arabic.[73] Immigrants brought many of their customs and traditions to the New World.[74] In turn, during the sixteenth century Mexico is credited with introducing to Spain and to other European countries three extremely significant court dances: the pavane, the sarabande, and the chaconne.

Scholars have different theories as to when and how the pavane dance became popular. Robert Stevenson in *Music in Mexico* notes that when Cortés returned to Spain immediately following the conquest, a group of entertainers and Indigenous dancers, who some scholars believe were an early band of Conchero dancers, traveled with him. Their dance performances and the dancers' beautiful headdresses, which resembled the feathers of a peacock, impressed the court of Charles V. In the eyes of the nobility, the Indigenous dancers appeared to be imitating the graceful, proud, and stately promenade of a peacock. A dance believed to be the pavane began following the visit;[75] however, some scholars no longer believe this

[71] Meyer and Sherman, p. 217.

[72] *The New Grove Dictionary of Music and Musicians,* XII (1980), S.v. "Mexico."

[73] Weinstock (ed.), *Mexican Music,* p. 10.

[74] *The Encyclopedia Americana,* XVII (1983), S.v. "Mexico."

[75] Stevenson, p. 94.

dance was solely of Spanish or Mexican beginnings.[76]

Famed Mexican composer Carlos Chávez states that the pavane was invented in Mexico during the sixteenth century.[77] In his *Dictionnaire de Danse*, published in 1787, Charles Compan also identified the pavane as being of "New World origin." Stevenson quotes Compan saying that the steps of the dance "mimicked the courtship routine of a turkey-cock making overtures to its hen."[78] In Italian publications of the period, this same dance was given the alternative titles of *padovanas*, *paduanas*, and *pavanas*. Because of this confusion in dance names, it is hard to determine exactly when these dances were introduced.[79] Giving credit to Cortés' Indigenous entourage for playing any significant part in the introduction of the pavane is contentious.[80]

In his *World History of Dance*, Curt Sachs indicates that both the chaconne and the sarabande began in the New World. He noted that the dancing of the sarabande was prohibited in Spain by legislation enacted in 1583, which Sachs took as the first record of the sarabande. Along this line, Sachs noted that "the singing and reciting of the sarabande in whatsoever place, was punishable with two hundred lashes; in addition, men were given six years in the galleys, and girls were exiled from the kingdom."[81]

Four years earlier, however, in 1579, Diego Durán, a Dominican friar and historian who compiled a history of the Indigenous dances, made note of the sarabande. This reference which is prior to 1583, the date considered as the beginnings of the sarabande, clearly indicates that the sarabande was not an Indigenous dance, although it

---

[76] Sachs, p. 356.

[77] Weinstock (ed), *Mexican Music*, p. 9.

[78] Stevenson, p. 94.

[79] Ibid.

[80] Ibid.

[81] Sachs, p. 367.

was danced by the Mexican-born Spaniards.[82] The sarabande was described by Durán as a vulgar and disgusting dance

> ...and still more different in type was another dance they performed which might have been derived from that lascivious sarabande which our own people dance with such indecent contortions of the body and such lewd grimaces."[83]

In the sixteenth century, the chaconne was a sensual and wild dance, but the sarbande was considered to be the most passionate and unbridled of all dances. Curt Sachs says that most old sources agree that the sarabande was a "sexual pantomime of unparalleled suggestiveness."[84]

Italian Giambattista Marino's lengthy poem, *L'Adone*, as interpreted by Stevenson in his historical survey of Mexican music, identifies and describes both the sarabande and the chaconne. He refers to these as twin dances imported from New Spain. To both dances Marino attributed "obscene motions and lewd gestures" suggesting "ultimate intimacies."[85] Dance accompaniment was provided by sensual finger snapping and *zapateado* rhythms (percussive foot/heel/toe stomping techniques), and by male dancers beating tambourines.[86] The sarabande and the chaconne were considered by Marino to be virtual "frenetic orgies accompanied by noise-making instruments."[87]

Sachs interpretation of Marino's poem is also graphic:

[82] Stevenson, p. 95.

[83] Ibid., p. 29.

[84] Sachs, p. 367.

[85] Stevenson, p. 95.

[86] Ibid., p. 95.

[87] Ibid.

The girls with castanets, the men with tambourines, exhibit indecency in a thousand positions and gestures. They let the hips sway and the breast knock together. They close their eyes and dance the kiss and the last fulfillment of love.[88]

Sachs indicates that New Spain (Yucatán) was the point of origin of the sarabande and chaconne. "It must appear fairly certain," he says, "that the sarabande with its unimpaired primitivism was picked up not in Europe in the sixteenth century but in Central America."[89] A poetic eulogy of the sarabande and the chaconne recorded in eighteenth century Portuguese *Cartas Chilenas* (*Chilean Letters*) uses the term sarabande jacara, "lundú" and "batuque" as names for the same dance.[90] A translation follows,

> The nimble mulatto girl dressed as a man
> Swings in the fiery lundú and batuque,
> Like the maiden who gracefully raises her skirt
> She flutters around on the tips of her toes,
> She opens her arms to the friend of her heart
> And presses herself against him: *embigada.*
> Her partner, winding and twisting his body,
> Now places one of his hands on his head,
> And the other he carelessly sets on his hip,
> Or snapping their fingers they follow the music.
> I'll pay you, I'll pay you, he cries, whereupon
> With a powerful leap he seizes the wench...
> Oh happy dance, into the lowliest huts
> Didst thou enter. The wives of the Negroes,
> And all the mulattoes did honor to thee,
> Their bellies grotesquely supported by girdles
> Together with rascals and gutter-snipes tattered
> Who shoeless would stamp in the dust of the street

[88] Sachs, p. 368.

[89] Ibid.

[90] Ibid., p. 369.

Yet today in the towns and cities of the portals
Of mansions and palaces open to thee.[91]

It must be remembered that these accounts are from the viewpoint
of the upper classes and not the peasant people themselves.

In 1599, the Spanish writer Simon Agudo included in a farce "an
invitation to go to Tampico in Mexico and there dance the *cha-
cona*."[92] In *El Amante Agradecido* (*The Thankful Lover*), a comedy
written by Lope de Vega in 1618, singers exclaim, "A jolly life, a jolly
life we lead, dancing the chaconne. It came over from the Indies by
mail, and now it dwells here in this house as its home; here it will
live and die."[93]

During the sixteenth century, the pavane, the sarabande, and the
chaconne dance forms had a significant impact on pre-classic music
and dance performed by and for European nobility in their courts.
For the first time *la raza cósmica,* the mixed race, invaded the dance
of Europe.

The African Influence on the Dances of Mexico

African people were present in Mexico from the earliest years of
the Spanish influence. During the conquest itself, about six Africans
were part of the Spanish force. Due to the expansion of the sugar-
based economy in the Caribbean, a substantial number of African
slaves were transported there, and eventually many of these were
taken to Mexico.[94]

Since African slaves worked mainly around the coastal regions
of the gulf and the plantation areas in the lowlands, the music and art
of both Africans and mulattos were injected into the Mexican arts
and moved into larger towns, mining centers, and other sites of hu-

---

[91] Ibid.

[92] Stevenson, p. 95.

[93] Ibid., p. 96.

[94] Meyer and Sherman, p. 214.

man gathering and industry:

> These included the emphasis on percussive rhythm; techniques
> of chant and response; the use of syncopation; scales of quarter
> tones; the use of frequently repeated short phrases; falsetto
> singing; and the source of the Indian marimba, an instrument
> coming to Mexico by way of Chiapas.[95]

From these roots, some of the regional dances and songs of Mexico
emerged and flourished.

There is considerable evidence of African influence upon dances
and dance traditions in Mexico. At the beginning of the seventeenth
century, the Africans established in Mexico City the custom of organizing public street dances. These dances attracted immediate atten-
tion and caused such disgust on the part of the citizens and the authorities that the Viceroy, Don Luis de Velasco, passed an ordinance
that prohibited public street dances by Africans.[96] The ordinance
written on January 2, 1609, stated,

> beginning today and until further notice, the black men and
> women cannot congregate in the street or anywhere else. On
> festive days, they may celebrate the occasion in the public
> square, and in no other location, beginning at noon until six in
> the evening, and they should return to their homes hollowing
> the festivity. If they disobey, by failing to return home or to stop
> their festivity, they shall be put in prison, given 200 lashes in
> public, and fined four gold pesos.[97]

The Africans and the Indigenous laborers shared many beliefs
and customs. Both regarded dance as an indispensable aspect of life,
and so it was not surprising that dance was interwoven with religion

---

[95] *Encyclopedia Americana*, XVIII (1983), S.v. "Mexico," p. 839.

[96] Gabriel Saldívar, *historia de la música en méxico,* trans. Sanjuanita
Martínez (México: Impresa Cultura, 1934), p. 220.

[97] Ibid.

and ritual. The polytheistic beliefs of both races included the worship of the sun god, both invoked their gods with melodic chanting, and both used a rattle and a drum for percussive effect.[98]

An entire century passed before the Africans were allowed to build their own churches or to practice their own faith, customs, songs, dances and rituals.[99] Often the Africans especially when they obtained their freedom, joined in the rituals and dances of the Indigenous people, regardless of whether such dances were Catholic or not. From the province of Panuco, Veracruz, a letter dated 1624 provides some evidence of this practice: "being that this dance is of an Indian superstitious pagan nature, it seems that certain Negroes, mulattoes, and *mestizos* dance it..."[100]

In the middle of the seventeenth century, the Africans began two forms of festivity in order to continue the practice and performance of their rituals: *oratorios* and *escapularios*. These festivities had religious content. The *oratorios* were of a solemn and religious nature, whereas the *escapularios,* introduced a decade later, consisted of festivities of a combined secular and religious form.[101]

These songs and dances were all accompanied by the guitar and harp and were performed by African, mulattoes, and *mestizos*. But the Holy Inquisition forbade these *oratorios* and *escapularios* because the saints were ridiculed and suggestive dances were performed.[102] In the General Archives of the Nation, Inquisition Branch, located in Puebla, there can be found documentary sources, dated 1669, that provide evidence of a variety of polytheistic religious festivities. In 1689, the Commission in Oaxaca denounced the *oratorios* and *escapularios* because the Africans substituted the words "godmother" and "godfather" for saints' names; furthermore, the dances

[98] Lekis, p.20.

[99] Saldívar, p. 221.

[100] Ibid., p. 220.

[101] Saldívar, p. 221.

[102] Mompradé and Gutiérrez, p. 42.

were considered indecent and the ceremonies to be of superstitious nature.[103]

One of the oldest and most popular African dances which was introduced from the West Indies was the *portorico*.[104] Another dance, the *chuchumbé,* a dance with chants, attracted the displeasure of the Holy Inquisition who, in the port of Veracruz in 1766, denounced it for being an indecent and dishonest dance due to features such as "swinging of the hips, touching of hands by the opposite sex, and holding each other in an embrace position with the stomach almost touching."[105] The *chuchumbé* was usually performed by the "low class, vulgar people, sailor, Negroes, and mulattoes."[106]

With the arrival of the Africans from Cuba in 1776, at the port of Veracruz, uninhibited dancing was reintroduced and found its new life in the *saraos* (social dance hops) of these African slaves. The *tango etíope,* the *danzas, sones, danzónes,* and *rumbas* that were popular in Cuba became the Africans social dances in Mexico.[107]

The authorities, concerned about the adverse effect these dances in which both sexes participated might have on public morals threatened to excommunicate those who performed and popularized these dances. The Holy Inquisition, in 1779, also imposed a six month prison term on any musician who accompanied these dances.[108] These threats, however, did not stop the dancing.

By the latter part of the eighteenth century these Caribbean dances had filtered into the social gatherings of the upper classes. The people of African descent and mulattos became the music and dance instructors in the larger cities of Mexico. They became the dance

[103] Saldívar, pp. 222-223.

[104] Ibid., p. 42.

[105] Saldívar, p. 227.

[106] Mompradé and Gutiérrez, p. 43.

[107] Ibid., p. 42.

[108] Slonimsky, p. 220.

masters of the elite and their music was interwoven with Indigenous and European musical influence.[109]

The prodigious rhythmic power of the music and dance of the Africans, introduced in the newly emerging nation of Mexico, added definite and distinctive cultural overtones. Even though they were initially feared, hated, and even prohibited, the rhythms and dances from Africa influenced those of Mexico.[110] The popular social dances of the *rumba*, and the *huapango* as seen performed today in the tropical, coastal regions of Mexico, continue to show their African roots.[111] The dances that originated during the period of the Spanish colonization were a tapestry of many artistic cultural influences that gave birth to the colorful *mestizo sones* that appear in the next era, 1810 to 1910.

[109] Mompradé and Gutiérrez, pp. 42-43.

[110] Lekis, p. 20.

[111] Stevenson, p. 96.

CHAPTER 4: DANCE IN MEXICO (1810-1910) - THE INDEPENDENCE OF MEXICO

The shout for independence, "Mejicanos, viva Méjico," rendered on September 16, 1810, initiated a dramatic change in the history of Mexico.[1] During the next hundred years, the government changed from a Spanish colony fleeing from a foreign monarchy to a fledgling democracy. Inexperience, however, doomed democracy in Mexico; soon the people were ruled by a dictator, native-born, but dictator nonetheless. The one hundred years, 1810-1910, were stormy. Revolts and crises caused political and economic conditions to rise to great heights and then to plumage to low depths.[2] Many patriots died defending their country's freedom. Among the most famous of these were Father Miguel Hidalgo y Costilla, whose dream inspired the revolution; Father José María Morelos, whose leadership helped change the country; and Vicente Guerrero, whose plans assured equal rights for the *mestizos*.[3]

Father José María Morelos, a solider from Valladolid, Michoacán, gathered supporters for his two objectives: to gain Mexico's independence from Spain and to establish Mexico as a Republic. In 1814, Morelos wrote a constitution abolishing "slavery, titles of nobility, government monopolies, sales taxes, and all forms of tribute."[4] This constitution guaranteed the people administrative rule by Mexicans, the right to elect their won representatives to Congress, and equal protection under the law.[5] Morelos' attempt to reform, however, was

[1] McHenry, p. 93.

[2] Duggen, p. 100.

[3] Smith, pp. 210-212.

[4] Ibid., p. 212.

[5] Ibid.

frowned upon by the Catholic Church, and soon he followed Hidalgo to jail. The Holy Office of the Inquisition found him guilty of heresy against the Church and treason against Spain. He was executed on the 22 of December, 1815.[6]

A *mestizo* who had opposed Hidalgo and had helped defeat Morelos, Agustín de Iturbide, allied with Vicente Guerrero. Together they wrote the Plan de Iguala, on February 24, 1821. The date is celebrated as a national holiday in Mexico, *el día de la constitución* (constitution day). The Plan offered inhabitants of Mexico freedom from Spanish domination and equality for Spaniards and creoles alike. The Plan also pacified the Catholic Church by guaranteeing supremacy.[7]

Iturbide officially proclaimed Mexico's independence on September 21, 1821, in the nation's capital. Less than a year later, on July 25, 1822, Iturbide established himself as Mexico's new Emperor, Agustín I, but his rise to power was short lived and he was succeeded by Antonio López de Santa Anna.[8] From 1823-1855, Santa Anna ruled intermittently as a dictator of Mexico. During his twenty-five year reign, Santa Anna managed to alienate his vice-president, both the Liberals and the Conservatives, the entire United States government, Texas, and most of his people. Many Mexicans consider him the traitor responsible for the loss of the great expanse of land from Texas up to Colorado and across to California.[9] Santa Anna was overthrown in 1855.

Ignacio Commonfort, the new President of the Reform Period, chose Benito Juárez as Vice-President. Juárez was unique: he was a full-blooded Indigenous Zapotec from Oaxaca who had studied the legal system and had become a lawyer. Commonfort and Juárez led the reformation to right the wrongs of the previous rulers. Together they helped produce the Constitution of 1857. This document guaranteed civil rights to all Mexicans and denied the Catholic Church's

[6] Ibid., p. 213.

[7] *Collier's Encyclopedia*, XVI (1981), S.v. "Mexico," p. 96.

[8] Smith, p. 213.

[9] Ibid.

right to its land holdings. The Church refused to recognize this Constitution and the pressure forced Commonfort to resign in 1858, at which time Benito Juárez became president.[10]

As President, Benito Juárez furthered the Reform Movement and brought about the "second true revolution in Mexican history."[11] In promoting the two principal elements of the 1857 Constitution, federalism and liberalism, differing ideologies clashed, and the War of the Reform began.[12] Juárez was in office for fourteen years. Because he strove to eliminate illiteracy, he is honored as the Father of Mexican Public Education. When he died in 1872, Benito Juárez, one of Mexico's strongest heads of state, was credited with leading the political reform, reconstructing a battle-worn country, and establishing strong policies against foreign intervention.[13] He died as a respected national hero.

During the Civil War in Mexico, the opposing sides confiscated property belonging to several European countries.[14] Eventually, England and Spain left the ports they had occupied. Napoleon III, however, sent troops to establish a French empire in Mexico. The Mexican army defeated the encroaching French troops on May 5, 1862, in the Battle of Puebla. The national holiday known as *el cinco de mayo* (fifth of May) commemorates this victory.[15]

A year later the French troops were refortified and did occupy Mexico City. Archduke Ferdinand Maximilian Von Hapsburg, a prince of Austria, and his wife Carlota became Emperor and Empress of Mexico. The intrusion by the French changed the form of government for which the Mexicans had struggled, and resentment among

---

[10] Fent Ross, *Made in Mexico*, p. 298.

[11] *Collier's Encyclopedia*, XVII (1981), S.v. "Mexico," p. 99.

[12] Ibid.

[13] Duggan, p. 101.

[14] Fent Ross, *Made in Mexico*, p. 298.

[15] *Collier's Encyclopedia*, XVI (1981), S.v."Mexico," p. 97.

some ran deep. "Mexico represented a New World in ferment. The Emperor and Empress represented the distilled traditions of the Old World."[16] Alfonso Teja Zabre, in the *Guide to the History of Mexico* writes that Maximilian Von Hapsburg was never an effective Emperor. Not only did he lack strength and assertiveness, but he also lacked knowledge of Mexican history, geography, customs, and struggles. He had no empathy for the people whose complex racial problems were monumental.[17]

Napoleon's withdrawal of support and military aid left Maximilian Von Hapsburg powerless. This, together with Juárez's supporters who continued their violent opposition to the empire, led to Von Hapsburg's defeat.[18] His army was captured at the Battle of Querétaro in June of 1867. At the site of this battle, on the *Cerro de las Campañas* (Hill of the Bells), Maximilian Von Hapsburg and his two general were executed after a court martial. The Battle of Querétaro is known as" the sunset of the imperial dream."[19]

Porfirio Díaz, an Indigenous Mixteca from the state of Oaxaca, came into power nine years after Von Hapsburgs' reign. His term in office was known for its "little politics, much administration."[20] Nevertheless, Mexicans elected Díaz seven terms as president from 1876 to 1880 and again from 1884 to 1911. He eventually became the advocate of justice, peace, and especially prosperity.[21]

Under Díaz's administration Mexico's economy stabilized. He established banks; promoted agriculture, mining, manufacturing, and commerce; financed the building of railways and telegraph lines; set up a national postal service; organized the *rurales* (country police

[16] Smith, p. 234.

[17] Zabre, pp. 315-316.

[18]Smith, p. 237.

[19] Ibid.

[20] *Collier's Encyclopedia*, XVI (1981), S.v. "Mexico,"

[21] Banks, pp. 409-410.

force); instituted public schools; distributed the land; and curtailed the absolute power of the church.[22] Between 1876 and 1910, Mexico grew into a cultural and intellectual mecca. Beautification efforts in Mexico City resulted in its being referred to as "the Paris of America."[23]

Unfortunately, however, the promises of Díaz's presidency fell apart as time went on. It became apparent that the improvements were benefitting only those few Mexicans already rich, the bureaucrats, and foreign investors. Díaz's policies became inconsistent as he pitted different foreign countries' interests against each other, a policy he also had long used in Mexico itself. As a result, when he was eighty years old, on May 24, 1911, Don Porfirio Díaz, the man who modernized Mexico was forced to resign the presidency.[24] This significant event put the long-standing hoped for "golden age" to rest. Díaz's "dictatorship with its good and its evil came to an end; revolution, with it horrors," awaited Mexico.[25] Not long afterwards, on July 2, 1915, Porfirio Díaz died in Paris, France.[26]

Mexico had waged war against Spain to gain its independence. It had then moved from being a fledgling Republic, to being dominated by French emperor, to being ruled by a dictator/president, back to being in the midst of a civil war. With Mexican pitted against Mexican, Church against State, rich against poor, drastic changes occurred. By the end of the nineteenth century, Mexico had changed so much from the beginnings laid by Juárez as to be accused of being "the mother of foreigners and the stepmother of her own children."[27]

Table Four presents a chronological summary of this period's

---

[22] Ibid.

[23] McHenry, p. 144.

[24] *Collier's Encyclopedia*, XVI (1981), S.v. "Mexico," p.98.

[25] Banks, p. 413.

[26] McHenry, p. 153.

[27] Ibid, p. 145.

most significant events. This outline is followed by a discussion about how the historical events affected the development of music and dance in Mexico.

Pictured above: Dancers of the UT Ballet Folklorico perform a few *sones* from the state of Veracruz, Mexico in the late 1970s. Photo courtesy of the Sanjuanita Martínez-Hunter Collection.

Table Four
Historical Chronology

1810   Father Miguel Hidalgo led the Mexican Revolution against Spain. The decree to do away with both slavery and the head tax was passed.[28]

1811   Hidalgo lost a battle at Guadalajara. He and other revolutionary leaders were captured and de-capitated.[29]

1812   In the Spanish Constitution of 1812 which lasted until Mexico declared its independence, the *jarabe* was mentioned.[30]

   The Catholic Church denounced *jarabes* for the anti-Clerical verses of their songs.[31]

   The Liberal Constitution was adopted; however, it was not followed by colonial officials.[32]

1815   José María Morelos was overpowered and executed.[33]

1822-1910   *Independence Period and Early Republic*

   Emperor Agustín de Iturbide (1822-1823)
   Vicente Guerrero (1829)

[28] Smith, p. 201.

[29] Ibid.

[30] Lekis, *Made in Mexico,* p. 51.

[31] Ibid.

[32] Smith, p. 201.

[33] Ibid.

Antonio López de Santa Anna
(variously from 1833-1855)

The Reform and the French Intervention

Reform Government – Ignacio Commonfort
(1855-1858)

Liberal Government – Benito Juárez
(1858-1872)

Conservative Government – Emperor Ferdinand
Maximilian Von Hapsburg
(1864-1867)

Post Reform Party

Porfirio Díaz (1876-1880 and 1884-1911)

1828 The Spaniards were ousted from Mexico
The Spanish fleet was defeated. Slavery was abolished.[34]

1835 Texas declared its independence from Mexico.[35]

1846 Texas was annexed to the United States. The United States
and Mexico went to war.[36]

1847 The *jarabe* became a popular song-form during the war between the United States and Mexico.[37]

[34] Ibid.

[35] Ibid.

[36] Fent Ross, *Made in Mexico*, p. 297.

[37] Lekis, p. 51.

1848   Mexico and the United States signed the Treaty of Guada-
        lupe Hidalgo. In it, Mexico agreed to the annexation of Tex-
        as, and sold to the United States most of the land between
        Texas and California.[38]

1854   A composer born in Spain, Jaime Nunó wrote the Mexican
        National Anthem.[39]

1856   Castro and Campillo's lithographs of scenes of Mexico and
        surrounding sites were published.[40]

1857   Pantomimes, burlesques, and melodramas regain populari-
        ty in Mexico. [41]

        The newly adopted federal constitution declared the sepa-
        ration of Church and State.[42]

1867   Mexican liberals made great gains in ousting French sol-
        diers by winning the battle at Querétaro, which led to Max-
        imilian Von Hapsburg's execution.[43]

1875   The greatest landscape artist of Mexico, José María Velasco,
        finished his famous painting "The Valley of Mexico."[44]

1884   Doroteo Aranga, better known as Pancho Villa, led revolu-

[38] Fent Ross, *Made in Mexico*, p. 297,

[39] Slonimsky, p. 221.

[40] Smith, p. 225.

[41] Ruíz, p. 57.

[42] Smith, p. 225.

[43] Ibid.

[44] Ibid.

tionary raids against the Díaz regime. Pancho Villa's battle songs, *La Adelita*, *La Cucaracha*, as well as, the waltz became popular.[45]

1887   José Guadalupe Posada, a social commentator, established a shop in Mexico City to sell his political cartoons and paintings.[46]

1893   Mexicans became irate over the *científicos* (scientists), an advisory group to the President Díaz headed by José Limantour, which opened the Mexican market to foreign investors. [47]

1910   The National University of Mexico was founded.[48]

In September, Mexicans celebrated their centennial. Indigenous art forms such as art, music, and dance were incorporated into the centennial celebrations.[49]

El Centro Artistico (The Artistic Center), the first Mexican association for artists, was organized by Gerardo Murillo, Dr. Atl (Náhuatl for water).[50]

1911   After eight terms in the Presidency, Porfirio Díaz resigned. Francisco Madero succeeded Díaz.[51]

[45] Slonimsky, p. 222.

[46] Smith, p. 225.

[47] Ibid.

[48] Ibid.

[49] Ibid., p. 251.

[50] Ibid., p. 252.

[51] Ibid., p. 249.

This year marked the beginning of the Mexican Revolution, a civil war.[52]

Pictured above are dancers of the UT Ballet Folklorico performing *El Son de la Negra* on campus during the late 1970s. Photo courtesy of the Sanjuanita Martínez-Hunter Collection.

[52] Ibid.

DEVELOPMENT OF DANCE

The struggle to gain Mexican independence between 1810 and 1830 changed the musical life of the country.[53] With the promise of independence, immigrants from European countries, especially Britain, France, and Italy, came to Mexico.[54] With them came influences from their own music and dance. Much of the musical folklore of Mexico was especially influenced by Spanish music and the Italian opera. The Spanish dances such as the *jotas, fandangos, seguidillas*, and *boleros* added diversity to the *sones de la tierra* (rhythms of the land) and to the popular music of Mexico. The *jarabe*, one type of *son* (song) which is typical of the spirit and gallantry of the Mexican people, was a direct result of this influence.[55]

After declaring independence from Spain, Mexicans naturally endeavored to alter those Spanish dances which had become popular in Mexico. The new executions of the *zapateado, petenera, malagueña*, and the Basque *zorzico*, along with the Spanish dances mentioned previously, differed from the original and were enriched by "the sensitivity and sensuality of the *mestizo*."[56] These popular Spanish dances and music became more and more Mexican in nature:

> The spirit of Romanticism and nationalism glorified "historical" and "folk" traditions within Mexico, thus reaffirming the growth of regional forms, such as the Gulf coast *huapangos*, the *sones* of the south, the *jarabes* of the western Plateau, the jaranas of Yuca-

[53] Béhague, p.96.

[54] Encyclopedia Americana, XVIII (1983), S.v. "Mexico," p.839.

[55] *The New Grove Dictionary of Music and Musicians*, XII (1980), S.v. "Mexico."

[56] Ruben Campos, *El folklore y la música mexicana*, trans. Sanjuanita Martínez (México: Publicaciónes de la Secretaría de Educación Pública, 1928), p. 108.

tán, and the *corridos* of the north.[57]

Since Mexico was no longer ruled by Spain, new elements contributed to keeping the ceremonial dances alive. For example, to celebrate the coronation of Agustín de Iturbide, on July 25, 1822, five lavish ceremonial dances were excitingly and dramatically performed. A tribe of Indigenous people from a village in Mexico danced in honor of the new Mexican ruler.[58] Another factor that intensely affected Indigenous ceremonial dances was the decrease in the power of the Church. Since the Holy Office of the Inquisition was no longer watching, dance troupes were free to incorporate the traditions of their ancestors into their creative choreography. Audiences grew in numbers and helped promulgate these new dances.[59]

New songs and dancers were also generated from special events which took place during this era. During the cholera epidemic in 1833, dances sprang up spontaneously imitating the painful facial expressions and the violent twisting of the body which accompanied the seizures associated with this disease. The *Telele* or Painter became popular among the common townspeople in Mexico. Soon, however, performances of the *Telele* were forbidden. It appears that as the epidemic spread and the dance became popular, new incidences of the disease were traced to the gatherings which viewed the performances.[60] Even today, "fits" of any kind are commonly referred to as *el telele*.

Songs and dances much like a gigue became popular in the *pulquerias* (town bars) during the nineteenth century. Mexican women who associated with the North American soldiers that had invaded the country were despairingly called *Margaritas*. At local dance halls, a satire set to music about a woman who mingled with many soldiers

---

[57] *Encyclopedia Americana*, XVIII (1983), S.v. "Mexico," p. 839.

[58] Covarrubias, pp. 34.

[59] Ibid.

[60] Momprádé and Gutiérrez, p. 45.

of the invading troops, La *Pasadita* was often danced.[61] At this time, a lithograph titled "Yankees y *Margaritas*" dancing a gigue appeared on a calendar. The 1847 calendar establishes the validity of the popular dance.[62]

Women in Mexico have been revered in music and dance since before the conquest. During the nineteenth century, the *China,* whose beauty and grace was comparable to Spanish ladies from Madrid and Andalusia, was the inspiration for the battle hymn of the army of Benito Juárez. Juárez's solider called themselves *Chinacos* after the young, unmarried *Chinas.* The brilliant red blouses worn by these Mexican girls were called *chinas*, the young girls were named for the outfits.[63] The elaborate beauty of the *China* outfit is described by Ruíz in *breve historia de la danza en méxico:*

> When Carlota [wife of Emperor Maximilian Von Hapsburg] arrived in Mexico wearing sequined dresses and fans and the Liberal and Conservative parties were formed, the *China Poblana* costume was modified to imitate the Empresses' fashion. White stockings with red shoes were worn by the women supporting the Liberal party; green shoes were worn by the women in the Conservative party. Sequins, resembling those of the Empress, adorned the skirts of the *Chinas*. Large gold or pearl earrings with matching necklaces or strings of coral beads in gold or silver chains were also worn by the women.[64]

The Inca term *Quecha*, which also means *China*, refers to a "household servant of the lower classes."[65]

---

[61] Ibid.

[62] Campos, *El folklore y la música Mexicana*, p. 108.

[63] Mompradé and Gutiérrez, p. 45.

[64] Luis Bruno Ruíz, *breve historia de la danza en méxico,* trans. Sanjuanita Martínez (México: Biblioteca Minima Mexicana, 1955) p. 49.

[65] *The New Grove Dictionary of Music and Musicians,* XII (1980), S.v. "Mexico."

Some of Mexico's most inventive minds planned the Revolution of Ayutla, the purpose of which was to remove Santa Anna from power.[66] This event give birth to *La Guacamaya*, (The Macaw), a political satire set to music. This *jarabe* sarcastically commented about the political situation in Mexico during 1854 and 1855 when Santa Anna and Commonfort struggled for control. *La Guacamaya* gave the people freedom of expression not only in creative dance but also in commenting about the country's politics.[67]

The French Intervention between 1861 and 1867 dramatically affected Mexico's political and economic stability.[68] To commemorate the execution of Maximilian Von Hapsburg and the escape of Empress Carlota, General Mariano Riva Palacios wrote *Mama Carlota*. The choreographed political satire with its cruel lyrics made clear Riva Palacios' bitterness about the French Intervention and its rulers. Whether or not all the people agreed with his sentiments is of no importance, for it was freedom to express their ideas that was celebrated in the *jarabe* by Riva Palacios. Within a month after its first performance, *Mama Carlota* was known throughout the Republic of Mexico.[69]

At rural gatherings and small town celebration, *jarabes* continued to be danced. Songs and *sones* were written for these celebration, but were no longer confined to these settings. Mexican humorists and romanticists from all ranks imitated the *sones* of the commoners and helped make them more popular.[70] Aristocrats composed original music, songs, and dances such as *Los Enanos* (The Dwarfs), *El Limoncito* (The Little Lemon), *El Guajolote* (The Turkey), *El Federal* (The Federalists), and *Los Aguadores* (The Waterers).[71]

---

[66] Meyer and Sherman, p. 373.

[67] Campos, *El folklore y la música mexicana*, p. 109.

[68] Meyer and Sherman, p. 401.

[69] Campos, p. 109.

[70] Ibid. p. 410.

[71] Momprodé and Gutiérrez, p. 44.

The Scottish wife of the first Spanish envoy in Mexico, Madame Frances Calderón de la Barca wrote *Life in Mexico* in which she speaks of dances popular in 1840: *jarabes*, *El Alforrado* (The Lining), *Los Enanos* (The Dwarfs), *El Palomo* (The Cock-pigeon), and *El Zapatero* (The Shoemaker).[72] According to Madame Calderón de la Barca, "The dances are monotonous, with small steps and a great deal of shuffling, but the guitar music was rather pretty, and some of the dancers were very graceful and agile."[73]

In *Los Enanos,* a popular song-dance *jarabe* in Mexico, an *enano* was represented by a dancer who "makes himself little" by squatting each time the chorus was sung.[74] Below is a version of the lyrics to *Los Enanos* found in Galindo's *nociónes de la historia de la música mejicana*:

Ay qué bonitos,
son los enanos
cuando los bailan
los mejicanos;
sale la linda,
sale la fea,
sale la enana
con su zalea.

Hazate chiquito,
hazate grandote,
ya te pareces
al guajolote.
Sale la linda...

Ya los enanos
ya se enojaron

---

[72] Fanny Calderón de la Barca, *Life in Mexico* (New York: Doubleday and Company, Inc., 1966), p. 221.

[73] Ibid.

[74] Ibid., p. 224.

porque a la enana
la pellizcaron.[75]

The translation by Sanjuanita Martínez-Hunter reads:

Oh how pretty,
are the dwarfs
when they are danced
by Mexicans;
out comes the lovely one,
out comes the ugly one,
out comes the female dwarf
with her sheepskin jacket.

Make yourself little,
make yourself big,
you already resemble
the turkey;
out comes the lovely one...

Now the male dwarfs
have become angry
because the female dwarf
has been pinched....

Fanny Calderón de la Barca omits the second verse in the version she quotes; however, she does mention that there are many more verses to *Los Enanos*. [76]

Church authorities denounced any music interpreted by men and women together, as having a degenerative effect on the morals of both the participants and the audience. Nevertheless, European salon dances became more and more popular in Mexico. The waltz

[75] Miguel Galindo, *historia de la música mejicana,* trans. Sanjuanita Martínez (Colima: El Dragón, 1933), p. 564.

[76] Calderón de la Barca, p. 224.

was one of these salon dances.[77] A Church official condemned the waltz as

> ...corrupt importation from degenerative France... All of man's depravity could not invent anything more pernicious, nay, not even Hell itself could spawn a monster more obscene. Only those who have seen the *Vals* [Waltz] danced with complete license are in a position to warn of its perils.[78]

Nevertheless, the popularity of the waltz grew during the nineteenth century. It was especially enjoyed at the social functions of Emperor Maximilian and Carlota. Soon, Mexico adopted the waltz as its own. An Otomí, Juventino Rosas, who lived from 1868 to 1894, wrote *Sobre las Olas* (Over the Waves). This great waltz was immortalized by the opera singer Enrico Caruso in its English version, "The Loveliest Night of the Year."[79]

The waltz was not the only ballroom dance introduced to Mexican society by the French; there were many: in 1830, the quadrille and lancers; in 1845, the polka; and in 1850, the schottische and the mazurka. Soon Mexican composers adapted the new rhythms to Mexican themes. French influence was strongly felt in Mexican music, dance, and fashion. [80]

Between 1830 and 1910 the salon dances were popularized and were enjoyed not only by aristocrats at balls, but also by common families at their gatherings.[81] Specific accounts of the musical ar-

[77] Slonimsky, p. 220.

[78] Ibid.

[79] Ibid., p.221.

[80] *The New Grove Dictionary of Music and Musicians,* XII (1980), S.v. "Mexico."

[81] Ruben M. Campos, *el folklore musical de las ciudades*, trans. Sanjuanita Martínez (México: Talleres Linotipográficos El Modelo, 1930), p.185.

rangements used to accompany these dances and the specific dances which were in vogue are unavailable in written records. At formal social functions honoring dignitaries, however, it is known that the aristocrats followed a precise program beginning with the honorary quadrille, followed by the waltz, the schottische, the polka, the *danza* (a Cuban-air rhythm), the mazurka, and the *dánzon* (an Afro-Cuban dance).[82] If requested by the host, the quadrilles consisting of the five Lancer dances and *Tagarotas*, were followed by the North American "Virginia Reel" and the program ended with the "Boston Waltz."[83] At times, during the aristocratic, social gatherings where there was no dignitary to be honored, less formal dances were also included in the program. These included the Czech *redowa* (a lively triple rhythm resembling the mazurka), the Polish *Varsouviana* (a variant of the mazurka), the Polish *Cracoviana* (a mazurka-polka), and the gallop which usually ended the dance.[84] At informal family gatherings many of these dances were included, however, there was no precise order followed in performing them.[85]

The quadrilles and *contradanzas* enjoyed by high society during the reign of Maximilian Von Hapsburg never became an important factor in the dance culture of the creoles in Mexico.[86] Parts of them, however, were adapted into several folk dances. The formations of the quadrilles, such as those where couples wove in and out of a circle as if forming a chain, are evident in modern folk dances. For example, in the folk dance *La Contradanza*, a musical satire on the ballroom dances of the Colonial period, twenty to twenty-four dancers use handkerchiefs or colorful ribbons in imitation of the aristocrats.[87]

---

[82] Ibid.

[83] Ibid.

[84] Ibid. p. 135.

[85] Ibid. p. 175.

[86] Lekis, p. 45.

[87] Arthur and Irene Warman, p. 745.

Other interesting formations from the quadrilles or *contra-danzas* have been adapted in folk dances where wooden hoops decorated with either flowers, ribbons, or handkerchiefs are used for effect.[88] In these modern folk dance adaptations new characters vary the dance patterns for the desired results. One of these characters is a *maringuilla* who is portrayed by an elder whose buffooneries entertain the audience. This particular folk dance has the musical accompaniment of one or two *huehuetl* players.[89] Although the costumes for the *contradanza* differ in each region, they usually include the flowery wooden hoops, the handkerchiefs, and/or the colored ribbons to augment the dance formations. Also, guitars and violins render diverse tunes to accompany the various dance patterns. Because this dance is similar to the Maypole dance performed at May fetes in Europe, its Indigenous derivation is often questioned.[90]

La Contradanza has become a popular folk dance in many parts of Mexico, from the Central Plateau to the mountainous regions of the Sierra de Puebla. On the second of February, during the religious celebration of Candlemas, the *Contradanza* is performed. It is also a favorite dance of many important community festivities.[91]

In 1864 when, at the request of some Mexican politicians, Napoleon installed Maximilian Von Hapsburg as Emperor of Mexico, many European customs became prevalent in Mexico, leaving little room for anything Indigenous.[92] While Maximilian and Carlota reigned, they held court in Chapultepec Castle. They invited European immigrants to their luxurious balls where guests danced "Viennese waltzes, Polish varsouvianas, French Cotillions, German schottisches"[93]

[88] Mompradé and Gutiérrez, p. 205.

[89] Arthur and Irene Warman, p. 745.

[90] Mompradé and Gutiérrez, p. 205.

[91] Arthur and Irene Warman, p. 745.

[92] Betty Casey, *International Folk Dancing U.S.A.* (New York: Doubleday and Company, Inc., 1981), p.201

[93] Duggan, p. 106.

and polkas, as well as, Czechoslovakian redowas. These dances continued in popularity even throughout Porfirio Díaz's later dictatorship of thirty-two years.[94]

Naturally the influence of these dances extended to different social strata. With many regional adaptations in choreography, form and manner, rural Mexico adopted the European ballroom dances.[95] In the northern Mexican states of Sonora, Coahuila, Nuevo León, Chihuahua, and Tamaulipas, the European influence gave birth to *música norteña* (northern music). In playing this music, a *redova* (wooden percussion instrument) keeps time and rhythm. The melody is carried by an accordion, and accompaniment is played by bass violins, harmonicas, and a *bajo sexton* (twelve-string guitar). In songs, lyrics are often in *corrido* (narrative ballad) form. In dances, the following forms are incorporated in the *música norteña*: polka, mazurka, redowa, waltz, schottische, *paso doble* (double-time rhythm or march), and *corrido* (running step).[96]

Between 1870 and 1900 salon music was published extensively in Mexico. Many Mexican composers allowed the European influences to inspire marches, potpourris, *boleros, paso dobles*, mazurkas, polkas, schottisches, and waltzes. The international flavor of the music was soon expressed in dance.[97]

Some, however, disapproved of the European influence in Mexican music; despite their efforts, however, the French influence on folk dances persisted, and the influence of Maximilian Von Hapsburg's grand balls cannot be denied. Examples include both *Las Mascaritas* (The Little Masks), from Mixteca in Oaxaca, and *Las Coloradas* (The Red Ones), from the Huasteca region of San Luis Potosí.[98]

---

[94] Stevenson, p.183.

[95] Mompradé and Gutiérrez, p. 46.

[96] *The New Grove Dictionary of Music and Musicians,* XII (1980), S.v. "Mexico."

[97] Stevenson, p. 206.

[98] Duggan, p. 106.

Las Mascaritas is a dance much like the Cotillion, with masks worn by the dancers to depict the French aristocracy. According to Anne Schley Duggan in *Folk Dances of the United States and Mexico*, the Mixteca Indigenous people learned this dance "as they peered through the windows to watch the French nobility dance during their balls."[99] *Las Coloradas,* on the other hand, is a dance much like the *Contradanza.* This particular dance re-enacts the political struggle in Mexico when some Mexicans sided with the French Imperialists. A male character in *Las Coloradas* is a Captain dressed in a French military uniform, a red dress coat with a white banner across the chest.[100]

When France sent her army to establish an empire in Mexico, the Zouaves were a part of the troop. The Zouaves were an army garrison that had fought in the Crimean War in which Napoleon had defeated Russia.[101] As part of their uniform, the Zouaves had adopted Russian boots. It is the Zouaves that are credited with the substitution of cowboy boots in the outfits worn by dancers in the *polkas norteñas.* While stationed in Mexico during the French Intervention, Zouaves wearing Russian boots helped add character to the style of *polkas, huapangos,* and *jarabes* by stomping their feet on the ground to emphasize the rhythm and movement of these dances.[102] There being no Russian boots in Mexico, these were replaced by the high-heeled *vaquero* (cowboy) boots worn in that part of the country.

In fact, it is a band of Zouaves that was defeated by Mexican soldiers in Battle of Puebla on May 5, 1862.[103] *La Batalla del Cinco de Mayo* is re-enacted annually in music and dance. The red-coated Zouaves (French soldiers) are defeated yearly by the Zacapoaxtlas people, armed citizens, and *Chinacos* (army troops). Many generals

---

[99] Ibid., p. 107.

[100] Arthur and Irene Warman, p. 744.

[101] Meyer and Sherman, p. 388.

[102] Mompradé and Gutiérrez, p. 46.

[103] Arthur and Irene Warman, p. 740.

take part in the mock battle. Costumes vary in the different locales from period military uniforms to lavish, fanciful clothes. Many times masks are worn by characters depicting both the Zouaves and the Zacapoaxtlas.[104]

La Batalla del Cinco de Mayo is performed particularly in Puebla and the surrounding towns,[105] but it is not limited to that area. For instance, in an old Aztec village called Peñon which is now within the city limits of the Mexican capital, *La Batalla* has been re-enacted yearly since 1920. According to Donald Cordry in *Mexican Masks*, the villagers of Peñon attended a performance of the historical re-enactment and found it so enjoyable that they decided to re-create it annually.[106]

Dance and the theater evolved together. The first classical school of dance was founded by Andrés Pautret in the early 1800s. Pautret had studied European dance and had grown to love it. So dedicated to his art form was Pautret, that whenever he found a talented pupil who shared his love of dance, he dedicated time and energy to perfecting the student's dancing skills and technique whether or not the lessons could be paid for. It was in Pautret's Academy that the famous Mexican ballerina, Soledad Cordero, made her debut in "Zefiro and Flora" in 1826. She gave a thrilling performance when she was merely nine years of age. Other famous works such as *La Niña Mal Guardada* o *El Niño Desesperado* (*the Unprotected Girl* or *the Desperate Boy*) and *Las Bodas de Camacho* (*Camacho's Wedding*), which was based on *Don Quijote de la Mancha*, were part of Andrés Pautret's repertory of spectacular dance works.[107]

Theatrical dance was popular from 1791 to 1794, but during the revolution not much thought was given to cultural advancement. In striving for Mexican independence, the public performances of French operettas and Spanish *zarzuelas* (musical comedies) were

[104] Cordry, p.228.

[105] Ibid.

[106] Ibid.

[107] Ruíz, p. 57.

squelched.[108] Theatrical performances did not flourish again until 1813 when the Viceroy Felix María Calleja came into power. The Viceroy loved dance and was a strong advocate of the arts. By attending the Teatro Principal for a testimonial performance honoring a well-loved Mexican singer Inesilla (Mexico's affectionate name for Inés García), the Viceroy sanctioned theatrical performances. To honor Inés García, José María Morales and Isabel Rendon danced *La Alemanda* (*The Allemande*), *El Jarabe*, *La Bamba Poblana*, *Los Boleros*, and *La Estatua* (*The Statue*).[109] Much to his delight, the Viceroy Felix Maria Calleja saw his first *jarabe* skillfully executed by Morales and Rendon, and listened to Inés García's distinguished rendition of El *Bejuquito* (*The Little Reed*), *La Indita* (*The Little Indigenous Girl*), La *Jaranita* (*The Little Guitar*), and *El Churripampli*.[110]

From these lavish theatrical presentations, new songs and dances filtered down to the townspeople who immortalized them by performing them at fiestas. The resulting musical style also became a part of aristocratic celebrations. Because the arts were then approved as culturally enriching, operettas from France and the *zarzuelas* from Spain again gained favor, especially in the cities.[111] Italian operas, performed by traveling European troupes of entertainers, became the Mexican musical horizon between the independence and the close of the Porfirian era in 1911"[112]

At the turn of the century, European musical styles continued to embellish Mexican "folk" music and dance. However, the "folk" music was transformed into an expression of Mexicanism as Mexico's independence became more well-founded. The longer Mexico existed in-

---

[108] Ibid.

[109] Ibid., p. 56.

[110] Ruben M. Campos, "el folklore musical de México," *Boletín latinoamericano de música*, trans. Sanjuanita Martínez (April 1937): pp. 139-140.

[111] Ibid., p. 140.

[112] Stevenson, p. 192.

dependently, the more national identity was reflected in its art forms. This national identity gave birth to the *son*, the national rhythm of Mexico reflected in its music and dance.

The *Son*-Mexico's Dance

Mestizo folk music was born from the blend of the Indigenous and Spanish cultures in Mexico. In the seventeenth century, a new variety of generic song and dance, the *son* (peasant song) appeared.[113] (Scholars today acknowledge the *son* as having *mestizo*, Indigenous, and African influences).[114] As the *son* became popular, those *sones* which were native to a particular locale were called *sones de la tierra*. By the nineteenth century, *sones* were identifiable as typically Mexican. *Sones* are popularly sung and danced throughout Mexico. The *huapango*, the *jarana*, the Chilean *son*, the *son jarocho*, and the *jarabe* are all *sones* which stem from the Spanish *zapateado* steps, dances, and music.[115]

When describing the *huapango*, the *jarana*, and the *jarabe*, it became necessary to differentiate between the dance itself and the accompanying music. Included in the account of a *son* is a description of the region of the dance, the costumes of the region incorporated in the dance, the complicated movements of the feet, the visual spectacle of the dance performance, and the instrumentation that accompanies each type of *son*.

Most *sones* developed from Spanish peasant or rural music.[116] A *son* differs from other music in its "form, rhythm, choreography, and

[113] *The New Grove Dictionary of Music and Musicians*, XII (1980), S.v. "Mexico

[114] Arturo J.Escalante Chamorro, *Mariachi antiguo, jarabe, y son: símbolos compartidos y tradición musicale en las identidades jalisciences.* (Zapopan: El Colegio de Jalisco., 2000).n.p.

[115] *The New Grove Dictionary of Music and Musicians*, pp. 231-235.

[116] Weinstock (ed.), *Mexican Music*, p. 9.

textual content."[117] Its characteristic "unequal triple rhythm" is based on "patterns of six beats."[118]

Independent couples dance *sones*, many of which are distinguished by the rapid action of the feet in a *zapateado*. The *zapateado* serves as accompaniment to the music when the rhythm of the dancers' feet produce percussion-type sounds. The *zapateado's* percussive accompaniment and many of the melodic instruments, such as the violin, stop while the lyrics of the *son* are sung. A *zapateado* produces its sound by the fast stamping of the feet on hard ground or on a raised wooden platform called a *tarima*.[119] As "one of the universal traits of the *son*," the *zapateado* is also a particular kind or type of *son*.[120] The *zapateado son* is danced primarily with a *zapateado* step. Many of the *sones* from southern Mexico which are accompanied by *marimba* music are generally known as *zapateados*. Many of these belong to the repertory of *sones de marimba* or *sones istmeños*.[121]

Lyrics for *sones* are usually written in rhyming couplets with eight-syllables in each line. The *son* usually opens with a dedication of the performance either to the gracious audience, to a particular important individual in the audience, or to beauty in individuals or in nature. The couplets of the *sones* often weave colorful tapestries of men and women in love surrounded by the beauties of nature.[122] *Malageña*, a love overture to a girl from Malaga in Spain; *Petenera*, a tragedy about sailors set to unusually lively rhythm; and *Indita*, a description for the passion of Indigenous women are three typical

[117] The New Grove Dictionary of Music and Musicians, XII (1980), S.v. "Mexico."

[118] Ibid., p. 232.

[119] Ibid.

[120] Ibid., p. 233.

[121] Ibid., p. 233.

[122] Ibid., p. 232.

sones that are appropriate for singing only.[123]

Different dance-type *sones* are usually accompanied by unique musical accompaniment. *Jarabes*, for example, are usually accompanied by a group of musicians known as *mariachis*.[124] *Huapangos, sones, jarochos*, and *jaranas* are accompanied by *huapangueros*. *Huapangueros* are second only to *mariachis* in popularity as musical ensembles.[125]

The *chilena* is a *son* that is danced in the Acapulco area in Mexico. Around 1848 Chilean sailors who came to the port of Acapulco introduced their national dance, *La Cueca*, to this area.[126] *Las Chilenas* (the Mexican version of *La Cueca*) is a dance in which couples perform apart from each other with the man pursuing the flirtatious woman. The woman coquettishly flaunts a colorful handkerchief while she dances. The *zapateados* of the couple become louder, faster, and stronger as the flirtatious actions end in seduction.[127] The *son Las Chilenas* can be danced to various tunes such as *Las Amarillas* and *La Sanmarqueña*. A musical ensemble of wind, brass, and percussion instruments together with a string bass accompany these dances. The Chilean *son* has spread widely throughout Latin America.[128]

The Mexican states of San Luis Potosí, Hidalgo, Tamaulipas, Veracruz, as well as, Puebla and Querétaro are part of the *Huasteca* region.[129] It is here that another dance-type *son*, the *huapango*, became

[123] Ibid., p. 233.

[124] Ibid.

[125] Ibid., p.233.

[126] Ibid., p. 232.

[127] Lekis, p.54.

[128] Ibid.

[129] Abrego Hernandez, Moises, 1998. "Hidalgo," in Asociación Nacional de Grupos Folklóricos Conference Syllabus, Aguascalientes, Mexico: ANGF. 52.

popular. It appears that the word *huapango* may be a combination of *huasteco* and *fandango*. A *huasteco* is a person living in the *Huasteca* region, and a *fandango* is a fiesta.[130] Another explanation of the origin of the word *huapango* is that it comes from the Náhuatl word which means on a platform or on a *tarima*.[131] A *tarima*, is the wooden platform on which *zapateado* steps are performed. The raised platform accentuates the percussive rhythm of these dance steps.[132] In Mexico, the *huapango* is second only to the *jarabe* in popularity as a *son*.[133]

There are different types of *huapangos*. In Tamaulipas, the *Huapango Huasteco* is performed in two lines of dancers on opposite side of the *tarima*. The dancers face each other, but show no interest in each other.[134] The dance is characterized by the precise *zapateado* steps with vigorous heel and toe stampings and the rigid almost motionless bodies of the dancers. In Tamaulipas, the dancers wear *vaquero* (cowboy) outfits complete with boots and cowboy hats. These dances are accompanied by a musical ensemble called the *huapangueros*, and by a couple of male singers whose falsetto notes resemble "the long notes held in Sevillian type of music."[135] The ensemble is composed of stringed instruments: "violins, guitars, *jaranas* (small double-stringed guitars) and in some regions harps."[136]

[130] Dickins, p. 10.

[131] Torres Del Ángel, Miguel, 2003. "La Huasteca Veracruzana," in Asociación Nacional de Grupos Folklóricos Conference Syllabus, Xalapa, Mexico: ANGF. 21.

[132] Weinstock (ed.), *Mexican Music,* p. 20.

[133] Lekis, p.51

[134] Ramon Valdiosera, *Mexican Dances* (México: Editorial Fischgrund, 1949), p. 2.

[135] Ibid.

[136] Covarrubias, p. 29.

A third dance-type is the *son jarocho*.[137] The *son jarocho* is danced with livelier, elegant *zapateado* steps and with the graceful air of the Spanish *seguidillas, soleares*, and *bulerias*. Mirroring the gaiety, lightheartedness, and energy, of the people of Veracruz, the *son jarocho* is a unique blend of their Spanish, Caribbean, and Totonac ancestry.[138]

The character of these *sones* varies from those like *Que Bello es Veracruz* where rich melodies are the main emphasis, to those like *La Bamba* and *Zapateado Veracruzano* where the main emphasis is the syncopation of the percussive rhythm of the *zapateado* steps. In some of these *sones jarochos*, trick steps are traditionally incorporated in order to add diversity. In *La Bamba* for instance, the dancing couple, using only their agile feet, forms the man's sash into a bow.[139] The *son jarocho* reflects African influences which are found in the Veracruz area. Veracruz was the chief slave-running port at the beginning of the sixteenth century.[140]

Accompaniment for the *son jarocho* is provided by the vibrato of the *requinto* and the *jarana*, guitars, and the harp.[141] The *zapateado* steps of the dancers provide the percussive rhythm for the music. Lyrics for these *sones* are often improvised satiric rhymes quickly created by anyone: the accompanying singers, the dancers, the musicians, members of the audience.

The tropical climate of the coastal region of Veracruz dictates the costume for the *sones jarochos*. The dancers wear light colored, light weight outfits:

---

[137] Ibid.

[138] Hernández, p. 45.

[139] Ibid.

[140] Jean B. Johnson, "The Huapango: A Mexican Song Contest," *California Folklore Quarterly,* July, 1942, p.235.

[141] Hernández, p. 45.

...a great flounced skirt, a small black, flower embroidered apron, a blouse and a thin, triangular shawl secured at the bosom with a brooch. The head is adorned with flowers, bows, and decorative combs.[142]

The male dancer wears a simple, elegant shirt, (*guayabera*) pants made of linen or cotton, and a straw hat.

The *jarana* is the fourth dance-type of *son*. The dance is named after the small guitar of the same name. The word *jarana* can be literally translated as "happy and vivacious." The *jarana* is much like the Spanish *jota*, a dance popular in Aragón. *Jaranas* are most popular in Yucatán, Campeche, Tabasco, and Quintana Roo.[143]

The Spanish *jota, zapateado*, and *seguidillas* of the 1600 and 1700 became popular in the Yucatán peninsula. The locals of the area assimilated parts of the new Spanish music into the aboriginal dances, and soon the *Jarana* took on a new "feel." The *Jarana* depicts the *mestizo* spirit like the *huapango* and *jarabe*.[144] Today the *Jarana* dances have diminished in popularity and are interpreted mostly by folk dance performing groups to represent the dances from the Yucatán peninsula.[145]

In Yucatán the townspeople, decked in their finest clothes, come together to celebrate a *vaqueria* (round-up) a traditional folk festival. The *yucatecas* (women from Yucatán) wear *gala* ensembles of lovely white *huipiles* or embroidered tunics, silk *rebozos* or scarfs, starched laces, and gold filigree necklaces. The men wear distinctive, white *guayaberas* also called *filipinas* (pleated dress shirts) with a short raised collar. Linen trousers, *alpargatas* (thick sandals), and fine henequen or panama straw hats.[146]

[142] Covarrubias, p. 29.

[143] Dickins, p. 10.

[144] Ibid.

[145] *The New Grove Dictionary of Music and Musicians,* XII (1980), S.v. "Mexico."

[146] Herrera Ochoa, José Rafael, 2007. "Yucatán," in *Associación Nacional*

The *vaqueria* usually ends with an elaborate presentation of a *jarana* dance.[147] The dance is directed by a leader who chooses the couple to perform. Men and women line up in rows facing each other to perform the *Jarana*. The sad music is danced with a fast hop step which interchanges with a much slower step that combines with the melancholy sounds. Throughout the *Jarana* the man pursues the woman while she flees to prevent any indiscretion. The couples dance for an indefinite time, and performances sometimes take on a marathon nature, lasting until the final couple decides to stop dancing.[148] The musical accompaniment for the *Jarana* is produced by *jaranitas* (small guitars), cornets, and kettledrums.[149]

Two of the most popular variations of the *Jarana* are the *Torito* and the *Colonté*. In the *Colonté*, dancers, with arms raised above their heads, snap their fingers in imitation of sounds made by the Spanish castanets. In the *Torito*, the male dancer uses his handkerchief as a cape in imitation of a bullfighter while the female dancer depicts the bull. It is the last version which is most popular at *vaquerias* (round-ups).[150] In other versions of the *Jarana*, dancers perform balancing acts, such as dancing with glasses full of water resting on their heads.[151]

Often, following a movement of music in the *Jarana*, the music stops abruptly to the shouts of "bomba, bomba!"[152] The dancer will then improvise lyrics much like the verse which follows,

de Grupos Folklóricos Conference Syllabus, New Mexico: ANGF. n.p.

[147] Ibid.

[148] Ibid.

[149] Valdiosera, p. 3.

[150] Covarrubias, p. 27.

[151] Valdiosera, p. 3.

[152] Covarrubias, p. 27.

> Me gusta mucho tus ojos,
> Me gusta mucho tu cara;
> Y si no fueras casada,
> Otro gallo me cantara
> ...Ah![153]

> I love your eyes
> I love your face;
> And if you weren't married
> It would be another story...Ah!
> (Literal translation, another cock would sing to me...)[154]

When the dancer finishes singing the newly composed verse, the musicians strike up a chord, and the music and dancing continue. The fifth dance-type *son* is the *jarabe*. The *jarabe* is not typical of the other *sones*; it is different enough to be treated separately:

> The *jarabe* consists of a series of musical sections, many of which have their own names such as *la diana* (a final section of most *jarabes*), *la iguana* (many have names of animals, which are mimicked in the accompanying dance), and *los machetes*. Each phrase of music is normally repeated, except the sung sections which are performed while the dancers rest.[155]

During the Mexican Revolution, the *jarabe* was banned for it was thought to be revolutionary music contributing to the political insurrection. The *jarabe* was first mentioned in print in 1789.[156] In 1796, the authorities of the Inquisition in the Catholic diocese of Puebla

---

[153] Toor, pp. 368-369.

[154] Ibid.

[155] *The New Grove Dictionary of Music and Musicians,* XII (1980), S.v. "Mexico."

[156] Saldívar, p.270.

publicly condemned a *jarabe* dance tune called the *pan de xarabe* (syrupy bread) for its lyrics were not in accord with the Catholic teachings.[157] They lyrics denied the existence of hell and devils. This *jarabe* was considered not only immoral but also suggestive:

> Ya el infierno se acabó
> ya los diablos se murieron,
> ahora sí, chinita mía,
> ya no nos condenaremos.[158]

The English translation by Robert Stevenson in *Music in Mexico* read in this manner:

> Hell no longer exists;
> the demons have ceased to be;
> come then my dear,
> no one will damn us.[159]

The first performance of the *Jarabe Tapatío* as we know it today was in the Coliseo in Mexico City on July 9, 1790. A Spanish clown dressed in a woman's costume at that time performed the *jarabe*.[160] *Jarabes* had an enormous influence on the Mexican people who quickly helped make the *jarabe* popular. Church authorities, ever-mindful of the deteriorating effect the *jarabes* had on the morals of the people, frowned upon the music, the lyrics, and the dance. By 1802, the performance of *jarabes* was forbidden by authorities of the Inquisition who issued a statement, [161] a part of which follows:

[157] Stevenson, p. 184.

[158] Saldívar, p. 184.

[159] Stevenson, p. 184.

[160] Dickins, p. 30.

[161] Stevenson, p. 184.

> Latterly there has been introduced amongst us another type of dance called the *jarabe gatuno* so indecent, lewd, disgraceful, and provocative, that words cannot encompass the evil of it. The verses and the accompanying actions, movements, and gestures, shoot the poison of lust directly into the eyes, ears, and senses. That lascivious demon, Asmodeus himself (Tobit 3.8), has certainly inspired this dance, so destructive is it of all Christian morals; but not only of religious virtue, even of the most elementary decencies. Its obscenity would shock even the most debased Sybarite...We are obliged by the character of our sacred office which pledges us to the salvation of souls by the blood of Jesus Christ, to prohibit, banish and extirpate this dance...[162]

The strong sexual content of its lyrics, the double-entendres in its language, the questioning of theological ideas, and the prohibition of its performance contributed to the ever-growing popularity of the *jarabe*. Its performances continued in defiance of the ban ordered by the Viceroy, Don Felix Berenguer in 1802. Rumors of the *jarabe's* insurrectory effects were confirmed at a hearing held by a court of the Inquisition in Valladolid on November 12, 1813. Joaquín Ponce, a choir director in the cathedral, gave sworn testimony at that hearing that the *jarabe* was "the secret revolutionary song sung at the conspiratorial meetings the house of a certain García."[163] Soon after 1813, the *jarabe* as publicly acclaimed throughout Mexico as the official song and dance of the Revolution.[164]

Original samples of *jarabe* music date to before the end of the revolution in 1821. The earliest of the *jarabe* music was played on guitar, but no record of written lyrics exist. Later in 1820 another *jarabe* was composed for piano. After the end of the revolution, some dance-type *jarabes* were written and signed by "name" compos-

[162] Ibid.

[163] Ibid.

[164] Ibid., p. 185.

ers.[165] Although the printed music was written for piano accompaniment, most often the *jarabe* dances were danced with *sones mariachis*. *Sones mariachis* were musical ensembles consisting of a flute, a string bass, a small guitar, and a harp.[166]

Mexicans fighting for independence composed the *Jarabe Largo Ranchero*. The *sones* of Jalisco were used as music for the *Jarabe Large Ranchero*. After fighting battles for independence, Spaniards and townspeople alike celebrated their victories by dancing this *jarabe*. People all over Mexico danced the *Jarabe Largo Ranchero* adapting it to new rhythms and adding regional characteristics to form new *jarabes*. Soon the performance of the *jarabe* was the ultimate expression of freedom throughout Mexico.[167] By 1862, the *jarabe* became so popular that the stigma stemming from its original ban was forgotten; it remains today in Mexican festivals.[168]

When Maximilian and Carlota reigned in Mexico from 1864 to 1867 the *jarabes*, which until then were considered a dance of the common folk, became accepted by members of high society. Over time, these "aires nacionales" were musically arranged to create the *Jarabe Nacional*. This dance would evolve and become known as the *Jarabe Tapatío* by the turn of the century.[169] In 1920, the federal government proclaimed the *Jarabe Tapatío* as the national dance of Mexico.[170]

[165] Ibid., p. 183.

[166] Ibid., p. 217.

[167] Mompradé and Gutiérrez, p. 44.

[168] Norma Schwendener, *How to Perform the Dances of Old Mexico* (New York: A. S. Barnes and Company, 1934), p. 3.

[169] Gabriela Mendoza-García, "Bodily Renderings of the Jarabe Tapatío in Early Twentieth Century Mexico and Millennial United States: Race, Nation, Class, and Gender." (Ph.D. dissertation, University of California, Riverside, 2013), pp 11-23.

[170] Flores Barnes de Angeles, Mexican Dance Symposium.

The adaptation of the *Jarabe Tapatío* as Mexico's national dance was significant for it symbolized the acceptance of the blend of the Spanish and the Indigenous people, and the acceptance of the true Mexican, the *mestizo*.[171] The *Jarabe Tapatío* is typical of Mexican folklore. Throughout the *Jarabe Tapatío* the courtship ritual is evident. The blend of Spanish and Indigenous cultures is apparent even in the costumes. The male *charro* outfit depicts the Spanish horseman adorned in Indigenous regalia, and the woman's *china poblana* costume depicts the Aztec legend of the eagle on the *nopal* (cactus) and the patriotism of the Mexican flag. The colors of the *china* skirt green, white, and red signify independence, religion, and union. The *jarabe* music, signifies independence and liberty. The *jarabe* dance itself embodies the character of the Mexican people their triumph over adversity, their passion for life, their virility, their color. Ruben Campos, noted Mexican musicologist refers to beginnings of the *jarabe mexicano* in his book *el folklore de la música mexicana* in this manner:

> La libertad había traído la alegría. La alegría necesitaba expandimiento. El expanidmiento de la juventud era el movimiento. Entonces surgío el jarabe mexicano.[172]

> Liberty has brought happiness. Happiness needed expression. The expression of youth was movement. Then the Mexican *jarabe* emerged. (Translated by Sanjuanita Martínez-Hunter)

As happiness, freedom, and independence spread throughout the young Mexican Republic, the *jarabe* embodied the folklore and character of the Mexican *mestizo* who has come to represent the nation.

[171] Ibid.

[172] Campos, *el folklore de la música mexicana*, p. 58.

CONCLUDING REMARKS

Mexico's history is reflected in its folklore which is uniquely expressed via its dance history, styles, and rhythms. A link between history and folklore is the dance. Dance development is affected significantly by important historical events and sociological factors. Miguel Galindo in the *historia de la musica mexicana* wrote about *music* what can be said equally about dance:

> ...la danza es la fiel expression de un estado social. La historia de la danza no es mas que una enorme sinfonia en la que se puede apreciar las harmonías con todos los timbres y motices que le dan los instrumentos de la orquesta social que se llaman raza puebleo, herencia, cultura, política, y religion.[1]

> ...dance is an honest expression of a social state. The history of a dance...[like] an enormous symphony in which one can appreciate harmonies with all its timbres and nicknames given to them by the instruments of the social orchestra which are called race, people, heritage, culture, politics, and religion.
> (translated by Sanjuanita Martínez-Hunter)

Dance in Mexico is an integral part of the people's folklore and I have shown numerous examples which indicate how significant historical events and sociological factors affect dance.

[1] Galindo, p.496.

SELECTED BIBILIOGRAPHY
Books & Dissertations

Bancroft, Hubert Howe. *History of Mexico.* New York: The Bancroft Company, 1914.

Banks, Helen Ward. *The History of Mexico.* New York: Frederick A. Stokes Company, 1926.

Calderón de la Barca, Fanny. *Life in Mexico.* New York: Doubleday and Company, Inc., 1966.

Campos, Ruben. *el folklore y la música mexicana.* México: Publicaciónes de la Secretaria de Educación Publica, 1928.

Campos, Ruben. *el folklore musical de las ciudades.* México: Talleres Linotipograficos El Modelo, 1930.

Casey, Betty. *International Folk Dancing U.S.A.* New York: Doubleday and Company, Inc., 1981.

Cordry, Donald. *Mexican Masks.* Texas: University of Texas Press, 1980.

Covarrubias, Luis. *Regional Dances of Mexico.* México: Fischgrund-Litographia Record, n.d.

Dickins, Guillermina. *Dances of Mexico.* Great Britain: Billing and Sons Ltd. Guilford, n.d.

Duggan, Anne Schley, et. al., *Folk Dances of the United States and Mexico.* New York: A.S. Barnes and Company, 1948.

Fent Ross, Patricia. *Made in Mexico.* New York: Alfred A. Knopf, Inc., 1958.

Fergusson, Irna. *Fiesta in Mexico.* New York: Alfred A. Knopf, Inc., 1934.

Galindo, Miguel. *historia de la música mejicana.* Colima: El Dragón, 1933.

Hernández, Amalia. *el ballet folklórico de méxico*. México: Artes de México, 1967.

Lekis, Lisa. *Folk Dances of Latin America*. New York: The Scarecrow Press, Inc., 1958.

Martí, Samuel and, Gertrude P. Kurath *Dances of Anáhuac*. Chicago: Aldine Publishing Company, 1964.

Mendoza, Vicente T. *la música tradicional española en méxico*. México: Imprenta Universitaria, 1953.

Mendoza-García, Gabriela "Bodily Renderings of the Jarabe Tapatío in Early Twentieth Century Mexico and the Millennial United States: Race, Nation, Class, and Gender." (Ph.D. dissertation, University of California, Riverside, 2013).

Meyer, Michael C. and William L Sherman. *The Course of Mexican History*. New York: Oxford University Press, 1979.

Mompradé, Electra L. and Tonatiúh Gutiérrez. *historia general del arte mexicano: danzas y bailes populares*. México: Editorial Hermes, S. A. 1976.

Peterson, Frederick. *Ancient Mexico*. New York: G.P. Putnam's Sons, 1961.

Ruíz, Luis Bruno. *breve historia de la danza en méxico*. México Biblioteca Minima Mexicana, 1955.

Sachs, Curt. *World History of the Dance*. New York: W.W. Norton and Company, Inc., 1937.

Saldívar, Gabriel. *historia de la música en México*. México: Impresa Cultura, 1934.

Slonimsky, Nicolas. *Music of Latin America*. New York: Thomas Y. Crowell Company, 1945.

Smith, Bradley. *Mexico A History in Art*. New York: Doubleday and

Company, 1945.

Soissen, Pierre and Janine. *Life of the Aztecs in Ancient Mexico.* Spain: Editions Minerva, S.A., 1978.

Stevenson, Robert Murrell. *Music in Mexico: A Historical Survey.* New York: Thomas Y. Crowell Company, 1954.

Stone, Martha. *At the Sign of Midnight.* Arizona: The University of Arizona Press, 1975.

Toor, Frances. *A Treasury of Mexican Folkways.* New York: Crown Publishers, Inc., 1979.

Valdiosera, Ramon. *Mexican Dances.* México: Editorial Fischgrund, 1949.

Von Hagen. Victor W. *The Aztec: Man and Tribe.* New York: New American Library, 1961.

Weinstock, Herbert, ed. *Mexican Music.* New York: Museum of Modern Art, 1940.

Zabre, Alfonso Teja. *Guide to the History of Mexico.* Austin: Jenkins Publishing Company, 1969.

Reference Books

Encyclopedia Americana, 1983 ed. S. v. "Mexico."

Encyclopedia Britannica, 1972 ed. S.v. "Mexico."

Collier's Encyclopedia, 1981 ed. S.v. "Mexico."

Funk and Wagnall, *Standard Dictionary of Folklore-Mythology and Legend,* 1972 ed. S. v. "Mexican and Central American Indian Folklore," by George M. Foster.

The Ephemeral and Eternal of Mexican Folk Art, 1971 ed. S. v. "La vida cotidiana de los aztecas," by Jacques Soustelle.

The Ephemeral and Eternal of Mexican Folk Art, 1971 ed. S.v. "Dances," by Arthur and Irene Warman.

The New Grove Dictionary of Music and Musicians. 1980 ed. S.v. "Mexico."

Periodicals

Campos, Ruben M. "el folklore musical de México." *Boletín latino-americano de música* III (April, 1937): 137-142.

Fent Ross, Patricia. "Regional Dances of Mexico." *Dance Magazine*, June 1949, pp. 10-13; 35-36.

Gallop, Rodney. "The Music of Indian Mexico." *Musical Quarterly* XXV (April, 1939): 210-225.

Génin, Auguste. *Notes on the Dances, Music, and Songs of the Ancient and Modern Mexicans.* Washington, D.C.: Smithsonian Institution, 1922.

Gillmor, Frances. "The Dance Dramas of Mexican Villages." *University of Arizona Bulletin.* XIV (January 1943): 17-22.

Jiménez, Guillermo. "The Art of Dance in Mexico." *Dancing Times.* August 2953, pp. 621-623.

Johnson, Jean B. "The Huapango: A Mexican Song Contest." *California Folklore Quarterly* I (July 1942): 233-244.

Sorell, Walter. "Mexico Cornucopia." *Dance Magazine*, August 1962, pp. 48-49.

Lectures

Angeles, Alura Flores Barnes de. "Mexican Dance." Symposium at the University of Texas at Austin, Texas, March, 1979.

Guerrero, Rosa Ramírez de. "Value Clarification of the Chicano Culture Through Music and Dance." Symposium at the University of Texas at Austin, Austin, Texas, February, 1979.

Photo of Gabriela Mendoza-García and Sanjuanita Martínez-Hunter taken in 2013.
This book is dedicated to the memory of Sanjuanita Martínez-Hunter.

ABOUT THE AUTHOR

Sanjuanita Martínez-Hunter earned her bachelor's, master's, and doctoral degrees in Dance from Texas Woman's University. A life-long educator, Martínez-Hunter began her career teaching physical education at Lamar Junior High School in Laredo, Texas and then at the American School Foundation in Monterrey, Nuevo León, Mexico. At these institutions she directed the dance teams known as the Lamar Prancers and the Monterrey Darlings while teaching at her own dance studio. Then, she taught at the University of Texas at Austin (UT) as a Dance faculty until retirement. Here, she was the faculty sponsor for many dance organizations such as the UT High Steppers and the UT Ballet Folklorico. This writing represents her doctoral dissertation which was completed in 1984.

ABOUT THE EDITOR

Gabriela Mendoza-García earned in Ph.D. in Critical Dance Studies from the University of California, Riverside. She is the founder and director of the Gabriela Mendoza-García Ballet Folklorico in Laredo, Texas. Her dance school and company performs traditional folkloric dance pieces, as well as, works that are inspired by her scholarly research. Her most recent publications include: "The Jarabe Tapatío: Imagining Race, Nation, Class, and Gender in 1920s Mexico" in the; *Oxford Manual of Ethncity and Dance*; "Creation, Growth and Inspiration: The Beginnings of the Asociacíon Nacional de Grupos Folkló-ricos (1974-1976);" and her dissertation entitled "Bodily Renderings of the Jarabe Tapatío in Early Twentieth Century Mexico and the Millennial United States: Race, Nation, Class, and Gender.

9 780692 099667